Annual Survey 2009

C000179769

US Government & Politics

Anthony J. Bennett

Presidential **election** 2008

Philip Allan Updates, an imprint of Hodder Education, part of Hachette UK, Market Place, Deddington, Oxfordshire OX15 0SE

Orders
Bookpoint Ltd, 130 Milton Park, Abingdon, Oxfordshire OX14 4SB
tel: 01235 827720
fax: 01235 400454
e-mail: uk.orders@bookpoint.co.uk
Lines are open 9.00 a.m.–5.00 p.m., Monday to Saturday, with a 24-hour message answering service. You can also order through the Philip Allan Updates website: www.philipallan.co.uk

© Philip Allan Updates 2009

ISBN 978-0-340-97282-3

First published 2009
Impression number   5   4   3   2   1
Year   2013   2012   2011   2010   2009

All rights reserved; no part of this publication may be reproduced, stored in a retrieval system, or transmitted, in any other form or by any means, electronic, mechanical, photocopying, recording or otherwise without either the prior written permission of Philip Allan Updates or a licence permitting restricted copying in the United Kingdom issued by the Copyright Licensing Agency Ltd, Saffron House, 6–10 Kirby Street, London EC1N 8TS.

Printed by MPG Books, Bodmin

Hachette UK's policy is to use papers that are natural, renewable and recyclable products and made from wood grown in sustainable forests. The logging and manufacturing processes are expected to conform to the environmental regulations of the country of origin.

P01390

Contents

Chapter 1

The invisible primary

What you need to know

- The invisible primary is the term used to refer to the year prior to a presidential election, before the actual primary elections begin.
- It is called 'invisible' because much of what occurs cannot actually be seen.
- The important things that a would-be candidate needs to concentrate on during this period are increasing name recognition, raising money and putting together the necessary state-based organisation.
- The media now plays an important role in staging intra-party televised debates between the would-be candidates.
- This is often thought of as the most important stage of the campaign, as often the candidate who leads in the opinion polls at the end of the invisible primary becomes the party's presidential candidate.
- This was not the case in either party in this election cycle.

The race for the presidency

The 2008 race for the presidency was littered with 'firsts'. For a start, it was the first presidential election since 1952 in which neither the incumbent president nor the incumbent vice-president was a candidate. This meant that both parties were starting from a blank sheet of paper when it came to candidate selection. The lack of incumbents always makes the selection more unpredictable and therefore tends to attract a larger field of candidates. By January 2008, there were 16 serious candidates for the presidency from the two major parties — eight Democrats and eight Republicans (see Tables 1.1 and 1.2).

These 16 major party candidates were noteworthy for including nine serving and former members of the United States Senate. Not since 1960 had Americans elected a serving Senator to the White House (John Kennedy) and not since 1968 had they elected a former Senator (Richard Nixon). Four of the last five presidents — Carter, Reagan, Clinton and George W. Bush — had all been former state Governors. But in 2008, only three of the 16 candidates had served as a Governor.

Table 1.1 Democratic presidential candidates, 2008

Candidate	Previous political experience
Joseph Biden	US Senator since 1973
Hillary Clinton	US Senator since 2001
Christopher Dodd	US Senator since 1981
John Edwards	US Senator (1999–2005)
Mike Gravel	US Senator (1969–81)
Dennis Kucinich	US Representative since 1997
Barack Obama	US Senator since 2005
Bill Richardson	Governor (New Mexico) since 2003

Table 1.2 Republican presidential candidates, 2008

Candidate	Previous political experience
Sam Brownback	US Senator since 1996
Rudolph Giuliani	Mayor (New York) (1994–2001)
Mike Huckabee	Governor (Arkansas) (1996–2007)
Duncan Hunter	US Representative since 1981
John McCain	US Senator since 1987
Ron Paul	US Representative since 1997
Mitt Romney	Governor (Massachusetts) (2003–07)
Fred Thompson	US Senator (1994–2003)

Momentum, media and money

During the so-called **invisible primary** of 2007, front-runners emerged in both parties. For the Democrats, the front-runner throughout the year was Senator Hillary Clinton of New York, the former First Lady. Clinton seemed to have so many advantages. She had name recognition. She had the Clinton political machine behind her. She had fundraising ability. She had the celebrity status of being the first front-running female presidential candidate for a major political party. And she also had what everyone described as her hidden asset, former president Bill Clinton. She maintained at least a 13 percentage-point lead over Barack Obama throughout the year. Indeed, by early November she had a 28-point lead over Obama (50%–22%) and a 35-point lead over John Edwards (see Table 1.3). The word used time and again about the Clinton presidential nomination was 'inevitable', and she played the 'inevitability' card for all it was worth. Hillary Clinton clearly had what the first George Bush had called 'the big Mo' — momentum.

Table 1.3 USA Today/Gallup polling of Democratic candidates, February–December 2007

Date	Clinton (%)	Obama (%)	Edwards (%)	Clinton lead over Obama
9–11 February	48	23	14	+25
2–4 March	44	27	10	+17
2–5 April	43	19	18	+24
4–6 May	45	27	14	+18
11–14 June	39	26	13	+13
6–8 July	42	26	16	+16
3–5 August	48	26	12	+22
7–8 September	45	24	16	+21
4–7 October	47	26	11	+21
2–4 November	50	22	15	+28
11–14 November	48	21	12	+27
30 Nov–2 Dec	39	24	15	+15
14–16 December	45	27	15	+18

While the Democrats seemed to be cruising to a Clinton coronation, the Republican race seemed to be an utter muddle with no less than five candidates all being seriously talked about as potential nominees. The campaign of the original front-runner, Senator John McCain of Arizona, had pretty much died over the summer of 2007. In August, his monthly fundraising fell below $1 million for the first time since he had launched his campaign. The former New York mayor, Rudy Giuliani, was the undisputed front-runner, maintaining a double-digit lead over McCain for the whole of 2007 (see Table 1.4). Only Fred Thompson's brief rise between June and October dented Giuliani's command of the Republican's invisible primary.

There was certainly more that was visible about the so-called invisible primary this time around. The most visible part of this stage of the nominating contest was the seemingly endless series of intra-party televised debates. The Democrats had scheduled 16 such debates while the Republicans came close with 12. With both parties having a large field of potential candidates the platforms at these events certainly looked somewhat crowded. Some of the lesser-known candidates found they were spending most of the time merely standing behind their podium waiting for a stray question to come their way.

Table 1.4 USA Today/Gallup polling of Republican candidates, February – December 2007

Date	McCain (%)	Huckabee (%)	Romney (%)	Giuliani (%)	Thompson (%)	Giuliani lead over McCain
9–11 February	25	2	6	42	–	+17
2–4 March	21	1	10	49	–	+28
2–5 April	18	1	7	42	12	+24
4–6 May	21	1	9	36	14	+15
11–14 June	20	3	8	29	21	+9
6–8 July	16	2	9	32	21	+16
3–5 August	16	4	8	33	21	+17
7–8 September	15	5	10	34	22	+19
4–7 October	16	7	10	32	20	+16
2–4 November	18	6	14	34	1	+16
11–14 November	13	10	12	28	19	+15
30 Nov–2 Dec	15	16	12	25	15	+10
14–16 December	14	16	14	27	14	+13

The other important activity of the invisible primary is fundraising. During 2007, Hillary Clinton raised more money than Barack Obama in 10 out of 12 months. Only in April and May did he raise more money than her. As Table 1.5 shows, she also out-raised him in all four quarters of 2007. And during the whole of 2007, Clinton raised $154 million to Obama's $129 million. Senator Clinton also out-raised John McCain, the eventual Republican nominee, in every month of 2007, often by huge amounts. For example, in September 2007 Senator McCain was able to raise only $1.6 million; Senator Clinton raised $14.1 million. Mrs Clinton clearly won the money primary.

Table 1.5 Money raised by Hillary Clinton and Barack Obama in 2007, by quarter

Quarter of 2007	Hillary Clinton	Barack Obama
First quarter	$36 million	$26 million
Second quarter	$63 million	$59 million
Third quarter	$28 million	$21 million
Fourth quarter	$27 million	$23 million
Total	$154 million	$129 million

In the Republican money-raising race, it was Romney, not Giuliani or McCain, who was leading during 2007. As Table 1.6 shows, Romney was the front-running money raiser in all four quarters of the year and had raised $112 million by the year's end, over twice as much as McCain. Mark Hanna, a nineteenth-century Republican campaign manager once remarked: 'There are two things that are important in politics. The first is money, and I can't remember what the second one is!' McCain might have suggested that what Hanna had forgotten was popularity and an ability to engage with voters.

Table 1.6 Fundraising by leading Republican candidates, 2007

Quarter of 2007	Mitt Romney	Rudy Giuliani	John McCain
First quarter	$23 million	$17 million	$13 million
Second quarter	$44 million	$36 million	$25 million
Third quarter	$18 million	$12 million	$6 million
Fourth quarter	$27 million	$14 million	$10 million
Total	$112 million	$79 million	$54 million

But what was utterly extraordinary about the 2008 presidential nomination contest was that so much conventional wisdom would simply be turned on its head. At the outset, conventional wisdom told us that the invisible primary is the most important part of the nomination; that whoever is ahead at the close of the invisible primary will — certainly in the Republican Party and almost certainly in the Democratic Party — be chosen as the party's nominee. Tables 1.3 and 1.4 show that, by mid-December 2007, Hillary Clinton and Rudy Giuliani had seemingly unassailable leads in the opinion polls, yet neither of them would end up as their party's presidential nominee.

At the beginning of 2008 there was little to suggest that the November election would not see Hillary Clinton elected as the first woman president of the United States, defeating the far-too-liberal-for-most-Republicans Rudy Giuliani. Mrs Clinton had 'experience' — that all-important ingredient which would surely be unusually highly prized in a year when America was at war and the incumbent president was perceived as being inexperienced, especially in foreign policy. What most observers, including the Clinton team, had missed was that voters were not looking for 'experience' in 2008 — they were looking for 'change'. And change, in the shape of Barack Obama, was just around the corner.

The primary calendar

Back in 2004, the two major parties had attempted to come up with a more orderly timetable for the holding of presidential primaries and caucuses. The secretaries of state for all 50 states had agreed to introduce a rotating regional plan. The nation would be divided into four geographic regions — East, South, Midwest and West — with the states in each region voting in March, April, May and June, with the order of the regions rotating every 4 years. New Hampshire and Iowa would be allowed to retain their 'first-in-the-nation' status, holding their contests in February. But the Republican Party sank the plan at its 2004 National Party Convention. So the result was the chaos upon which we commented in the 2008 Annual Survey (see Chapter 1,

'Primary chaos'). As a result, 38 states staged presidential primaries and caucuses before the end of February, the worst case of 'front loading' ever seen in the nomination calendar. On 5 February alone, there were contests in 24 states. By this date 55% of delegates to both National Party Conventions had already been selected. By the end of February, 70% of Democratic delegates and 68% of Republican delegates had already been selected (see Table 1.7).

Table 1.7 Number of nominating contests and accumulation of delegates, 2008

Date	Democratic			Republican		
	Number of contests	Number of delegates	Cumulative % of delegates	Number of contests	Number of delegates	Cumulative % of delegates
3 January	1	57	1.41	1	40	1.68
5 January	0	0	1.41	1	14	2.27
8 January	1	30	2.15	1	12	2.77
15 January	1	0	2.15	1	30	4.03
19 January	1	34	2.99	2	58	6.47
26 January	1	54	4.32	0	0	6.47
29 January	1	0	4.32	1	57	8.87
1 February	0	0	4.32	1	21	9.75
5 February	22	2257	55.74	25	1081	55.17
9 February	3	204	60.78	3	126	60.46
10 February	1	32	61.57	0	0	60.46
12 February	3	239	67.47	3	119	65.46
19 February	2	121	70.46	1	40	67.14
4 March	4	446	81.48	4	265	79.62
8 March	1	18	81.92	0	0	79.62
11 March	1	40	82.91	1	39	81.64
22 April	1	187	87.53	1	74	85.13
6 May	2	219	93.16	2	126	90.42
13 May	1	39	94.12	0	0	90.42
16 May	0	0	94.12	1	20	91.26
20 May	2	125	97.21	2	75	94.41
27 May	0	0	97.21	1	32	95.76
3 June	2	48	99.95	2	59	98.24

The main advantage of front loading is said to be that the party settles its nomination early, thus avoiding a protracted and expensive battle lasting for months. Unfortunately this advantage failed to play out for the Democrats in 2008. The main disadvantages of front loading are said to be two-fold. First, it unfairly favours well-known, well-organised and well-financed candidates and makes it much more difficult for so-called insurgent candidacies — such as that of Jimmy Carter in the 1976 Democratic race — to be successful. Second, because the nomination is decided so early, there is little opportunity for any reassessment of a candidate's potential weaknesses. A candidate can get swept into the front-runner position in a matter of weeks — even days — and by the time voters and the party hierarchy begin to perceive flaws in the candidate, it is too late. This situation is often referred to as 'buyer's remorse' — akin to buying something on impulse, only to regret the purchase shortly afterwards once the product is perceived not to live up to expectations.

The dramatic move towards front loading has also led to a chaotic timetable of primaries and caucuses with states thousands of miles apart voting on the same day. This makes it exceedingly difficult for candidates to campaign effectively in each state without having to travel thousands of miles as they continually criss-cross the country. For example, on 19 January there were Republican contests in both Nevada and South Carolina, while on 19 February there were contests for both parties in Washington state and in Wisconsin. Considering how events unfolded for the Democrats in their 2008 nomination race, reform of the nominating calendar is bound to take centre stage in the planning for 2012.

Questions

1 Define the term 'invisible primary'.
2 What does a potential candidate need to concentrate on during this period?
3 Why was there such a large field of candidates for both parties in the 2008 presidential contest?
4 What was unusual about the political background of many of the presidential candidates?
5 Hillary Clinton was thought to have five advantages going into the Democratic nomination race. What were they?
6 Comment on Hillary Clinton's performance in polls during 2007 when rated against her main Democratic rivals.
7 Who was the Republican front-runner during 2007?
8 How many intra-party television debates were held during 2007?
9 Comment on the fundraising by both parties' leading candidates during 2007.
10 Give some statistics to show how quickly the majority of delegates were chosen during the 2008 primaries and caucuses in both parties.
11 What are said to be the main advantages and disadvantages of 'front loading'?

Chapter 2

The 2008 Republican primaries

What you need to know

- Presidential primaries are state-based elections held between January and June of the presidential election year.
- They give ordinary voters a chance to say who they would like to be the party's candidate in the upcoming presidential election.
- The primaries also choose delegates to go to the National Party Conventions held in late summer, which is where the final decision about the candidate is made.
- Some small, sparsely-populated states hold caucuses rather than a primary.
- In 2008, more states than ever before scheduled their primaries or caucuses early in the year, a process known as 'front loading'.

The candidates

For the third time since the passage of the 22nd Amendment limiting presidents to two terms in office, the Republicans had a term-limited president who could not be a candidate in the forthcoming election. They had been in the same situation in 1960 when Dwight Eisenhower was ineligible for re-election and again in 1988 when Ronald Reagan had completed his two terms in office. But in both of those years, the incumbent vice-president — respectively Richard Nixon and George H. W. Bush — had sought and won the party's presidential nomination. But in 2008, Vice-President Dick Cheney had no interest in running for the presidency, thus leaving the field even more open than usual.

Table 2.1 Republican presidential candidates

Candidate	Date entered race	Date left race
Senator Sam Brownback	20 January 2007	19 October, 2007
Congressman Duncan Hunter	25 January 2007	19 January, 2008
Ex-Governor Mike Huckabee	28 January 2007	4 March, 2008
Ex-Mayor Rudy Giuliani	5 February 2007	30 January, 2008
Ex-Governor Mitt Romney	13 February 2007	7 February, 2008
Congressman Ron Paul	12 March 2007	12 June, 2008
Senator John McCain	**25 April 2007**	**Eventual nominee**
Ex-Senator Fred Thompson	5 September 2007	22 January, 2008

The Republican field grew during 2007 to number eight candidates — two serving Senators plus one ex-Senator, two ex-Governors plus one ex-Mayor, plus two serving members of the House of Representatives (see Table 2.1). But these eight would-be candidates could be divided into a first and second tier. The first-tier candidates were Senator John McCain of Arizona, the former Senator from Tennessee Fred Thompson, the former Governor of Massachusetts Mitt Romney and the front-runner and former Mayor of New York, Rudy Giuliani. In the second tier came the former Governor of Arkansas Mike Huckabee, Senator Sam Brownback of Kansas and Congressmen Duncan Hunter of California and Ron Paul of Texas.

At the start of 2007, the presumed front-runner for the Republican nomination was the Arizonan Senator John McCain. He had unsuccessfully contested the presidential nomination in 2000, losing to George W. Bush, but only after having resoundingly beaten Bush in the New Hampshire primary by 18 percentage points — 49% to 31%. This time around, McCain's two strengths were that he had ploughed an independent furrow during the 8 years of the Bush administration and his compelling life story as a prisoner of war in Vietnam for 5 years, during which time he was subjected to torture. However, McCain had two significant weaknesses to overcome — his whole-hearted, though not uncritical, support for Bush's unpopular war in Iraq, and his age. If elected, McCain would be 72 on inauguration day, making him the oldest ever elected first-term president. Reagan was 69 at his first inauguration in 1981.

If McCain were to falter, there were two potential beneficiaries — Mitt Romney and Rudy Giuliani. As CEO of the 2002 Winter Olympics in Salt Lake City, Romney had proved himself a successful businessman and competent executive. On the back of this, he was elected as Governor of Massachusetts — a Republican in possibly the most Democratic state in the nation. To these professional qualities, Romney added personable good looks. But he had two main drawbacks. First, there was a possibility that he might be seen as too liberal by many within the Republican Party, and coming from Massachusetts would not be seen as much of an advantage. Memories would be revived of another Massachusetts Governor and failed presidential candidate — Democrat Michael Dukakis in 1988. Second, Romney is a practising Mormon, not a sect which endears itself to the evangelical Christian wing of the Republican Party.

Rudy Giuliani had served as Mayor of New York City for 8 years between January 1994 and December 2001. But the events in New York on 11 September 2001, just a few months before he left office, thrust him into the national spotlight in a way that he could never have imagined. His courage and resilience on that calamitous day endeared him not only to New Yorkers but to millions of Americans. He was dubbed 'America's Mayor'. However, as with

Romney, there were many in the Republican Party who would find it difficult to support his liberal position on social issues, and his private life was colourful, to say the least.

The fourth top-tier candidate was Fred Thompson, the former Senator from Tennessee and more recently a star of film and television. He had played New York City District Attorney Arthur Branch in the NBC television series *Law and Order* as well as appearing in more than 20 films, including *The Hunt for Red October* (1990) and *Bury My Heart at Wounded Knee* (2007), where he played President Ulysses Grant. However, Thompson dithered over his entry into the race, leaving it too late to make any significant impression. He lasted less than 5 months as a candidate.

The Iowa caucuses

Even before the Republican primaries and caucuses began, Rudy Giuliani had made a decision that would scupper his campaign for good. Knowing that his kind of liberal Republican views would not play well in the early caucus and primary states, Giuliani decided to sit out the first six contests — including Iowa and New Hampshire — and concentrate all his resources on Florida, which had scheduled its primary for 29 January. But what Giuliani failed to realise was that the early states are critical for building up momentum. They are also important for gaining media attention. Giuliani gained neither.

This meant that the Iowa caucuses on 3 January were a golden opportunity for Mitt Romney to score the first win of the nomination season. Romney had been ahead in the polls in Iowa from mid-May to early December. By September, he enjoyed a 17-point lead over Rudy Giuliani. But Mike Huckabee, the former Governor of Arkansas, had come through with a late surge. Back in October, Huckabee was registering just 8% in Iowa polling and was in fifth place. The early stages of the nomination race are all about living up to expectations, so for Romney to lose to Huckabee would be a huge hit for Romney. Therefore, Romney spent the final days before voting playing down expectations.

Mike Huckabee did indeed score a major upset, winning 34% of the vote and leaving Romney in second place with only 25%.

The Iowa result (see Table 2.2) was a huge disappointment to Mitt Romney, who had virtually lived in the state for the past year and had spent millions of dollars in advertising there. His strategy had been to start with an impressive win in Iowa in the hope that this would translate into a follow-up win in New Hampshire the following week, which would in turn make him the undisputed front-runner before a showdown with Giuliani in Florida.

Table 2.2 Results of Republican primaries and caucuses, 2008 (winner's figures are in bold; (C) indicates caucuses; (SC) indicates State Convention)

Date	State	McCain (%)	Giuliani (%)	Romney (%)	Huckabee (%)	Thompson (%)	Paul (%)
3 January	Iowa (C)	13	3	25	**34**	13	10
5 January	Wyoming (C)	–	–	**67**	–	25	–
8 January	New Hampshire	**37**	9	32	11	1	8
15 January	Michigan	30	3	**39**	16	4	6
19 January	Nevada (C)	13	4	**51**	8	8	13
	South Carolina	**33**	2	15	30	16	4
29 January	Florida	**36**	15	31	13		1
1 February	Maine (C)	21		**52**	6		18
5 February	Alabama	37		18	**41**		3
	Alaska (C)	16		**44**	22		17
	Arizona	**47**		35	9		4
	Arkansas	20		14	**60**		5
	California	**42**		35	12		4
	Colorado (C)	18		**60**	13		8
	Connecticut	**52**		33	7		4
	Delaware	**45**		33	15		3
	Georgia	32		30	**34**		3
	Illinois	**47**		29	16		5
	Massachusetts	41		**51**	4		3
	Minnesota (C)	22		**41**	20		16
	Missouri	**33**		29	32		4
	Montana	22		**38**	15		25
	New Jersey	**55**		28	8		5
	New York	**52**		28	11		6
	North Dakota (C)	23		**36**	20		21
	Oklahoma	**37**		25	33		3
	Tennessee	32		24	**34**		6
	Utah	5		**89**	1		3
	West Virginia (SC)	1		47	**52**		0
9 February	Kansas (C)	24			**60**		11
	Louisiana (C)	42			**43**		5
12 February	District of Columbia	**68**			16		8
	Maryland	**55**			29		6
	Virginia	**50**			41		4

Date	State	McCain (%)	Giuliani (%)	Romney (%)	Huckabee (%)	Thompson (%)	Paul (%)
19 February	Washington	49			24		8
	Wisconsin	55			37		5
4 March	Ohio	60			31		5
	Rhode Island	65			22		7
	Texas	51			38		7
	Vermont	71			14		7
11 March	Mississippi	79			13		4
22 April	Pennsylvania	73			11		16
6 May	Indiana	78			10		8
	North Carolina	74			12		7
13 May	Nebraska	87			–		13
	West Virginia	76			10		5
20 May	Kentucky	72			8		7
	Oregon	81			–		14
27 May	Idaho	70					24
3 June	New Mexico	86					14
	South Dakota	70					17

In his article in the *New York Times* on 4 January 2008, David Brooks suggested three reasons for Huckabee's win. First, Huckabee represented a new strand of evangelical Republicans in America. Unlike most of his predecessors, he was not at war with modern culture — he plays in a band and has an ironic sense of humour. Second, Huckabee understood, in a way in which Romney did not, that many Americans have lost faith in their leaders' ability to respond to the problems which the country faces. Stated Brooks: 'While Romney embodies the leadership class, Huckabee went after it.' He criticised Wall Street financiers. He criticised K Street lobbyists. He even took on other conservative leaders and opinion-shapers — George W. Bush and Rush Limbaugh. Third, Huckabee seemed to realise that people's wellbeing isn't just about wages (as the Democrats suggest) or just about family values (as Republicans tend to suggest) but the inter-relationship between the two. Huckabee suggested, for example, that Americans' long-term prospects are much more likely to be damaged by divorce — and therefore having to live as a single parent — than by the outsourcing of jobs.

Huckabee's win in Iowa brought him an injection of money, media coverage and popular support. Among Republicans, Huckabee jumped from 16% support in December to 25% immediately after Iowa. Indeed, in the 4–6 January Gallup Poll, Huckabee was the Republican front-runner (25%) with Giuliani on 20% and McCain on 19%. Romney had fallen from third place in December to fifth with just 9%.

The New Hampshire primary

New Hampshire Republicans voted 5 days after Iowa. Between these two events, Wyoming held caucuses, but as neither McCain, Giuliani nor Huckabee contested them, Romney's victory passed virtually unnoticed. Not so the New Hampshire victory of John McCain. For someone whose campaign was left for dead just 6 months earlier, this was an extraordinary comeback. Mindful that back in 1992, Bill Clinton had described his performance in the New Hampshire Democratic primary as that of 'the comeback kid', the 71-year-old McCain remarked dryly in that night's victory speech: 'I'm past the age when I can claim the noun "kid", no matter what adjective precedes it, but tonight we sure showed them what a comeback looks like.' For a candidate who had raised only $16 million in the last 6 months of 2007 — Romney had raised $45 million in the same period — this was extraordinary. McCain beat Romney by over 5 percentage points and this, coupled with his Iowa defeat, was a bitter blow to Romney's campaign from which he never really recovered.

Exit polls showed how complete McCain's victory had been. He beat Romney among male and female voters and among poor and wealthy voters. He beat Romney among all age groups except his own — the over 65s — who gave Romney a majority of their votes. He even beat Romney and Huckabee among white evangelical Christians. McCain did particularly well among the independent voters who made up 37% of the Republican primary voters. Among this group, McCain won 40% of the vote to Romney's 27% and Huckabee's 9%. In ideological groups, McCain won among liberal and moderate voters but Romney came out top among conservatives.

From New Hampshire to Super Tuesday

During the next 4 weeks — in the period between the New Hampshire primary (8 January) and Super Tuesday (5 February) — there were five Republican contests: Michigan, Nevada, South Carolina, Florida and Maine. Romney chalked up his first win in Michigan, where his father had been Governor between 1963 and 1969. He also won the caucuses in Nevada, but as the only Republican candidate to have competed there, the win was regarded as insignificant.

The most important of these five contests was in South Carolina, the state that had delivered a death-blow to McCain's 2000 presidential bid. Now McCain needed to beat the new insurgent candidate, Mike Huckabee, who would find this southern state with its high proportion of white, evangelical Christian voters — 55% of Republican primary voters described themselves as such — very much to his liking. McCain won by a 3 percentage-point margin over Huckabee. Huckabee won among poorer voters — those earning less than $50,000 a year. He beat McCain 41–19 among 'very conservative' voters and 43–27 among white, evangelical Christians. Huckabee also won the majority of late-deciding voters. McCain's great strength — and possibly the deciding factor in his winning — was his support among independents, who accounted for 18% of the voters in this Republican primary. Among them, McCain won 42% of the vote to Huckabee's 25%. So, with Romney fading fast and Giuliani yet to surface, the Republican race was already taking shape as a contest between McCain and Huckabee. Could McCain appeal sufficiently to social conservatives within the Republican base? Could Huckabee broaden his appeal outside his conservative, evangelical base? Fred Thompson, who had made a belated bid for the nomination, came in a distant third with just 16% of the vote and quit the race 3 days later.

The Florida primary at the end of January would have taken on a greater importance if the Republican National Committee had not punished the Florida Republican Party for holding its primary before the sanctioned date of 5 February by removing half of its delegates. Nonetheless, Florida was important for Rudy Giuliani as he had based his whole strategy on victory in the state. It was a complete disaster for the former New York mayor, who came in a distant third with just 15% of the vote and exited from the race the following day.

This was an extraordinary and ignominious end to a candidacy that had promised so much. Giuliani had spent $63 million and gained not a single delegate. The winner in Florida was again John McCain with 36%. This time it was Romney rather than Huckabee who came in second with 31%. Romney had been ahead in the Florida polls right up to the penultimate week of the campaign, but after the popular Republican Governor of the state, Charlie Crist, endorsed McCain, Romney surrendered the lead. Romney took a consolation prize by winning the Maine caucuses 3 days later. So, as the race moved towards Super Tuesday, the Republican contest was down to a three-horse race — McCain, Romney and Huckabee. The question about to be answered was: 'Who would garner the most of the anyone-but-McCain votes?'

Super Tuesday and beyond

Super Tuesday was earlier and bigger than any of its six predecessors. Begun in 1984, previous Super Tuesdays had never been held earlier than 2 March and had never featured more than ten contests. In 2008, Super Tuesday was held on 5 February and featured 21 Republican contests — from Alaska to Alabama, California to Connecticut. This was meant to be the day when the Democrats crowned Hillary Clinton as their nominee and the Republicans were left with a horse race all the way to June. What happened was the reverse: the Republicans virtually crowned John McCain as their nominee and it was the Democrats who were left with a horse race all the way to June.

McCain wrapped things up on Super Tuesday, mainly by winning six of the seven winner-take-all contests, including California with 173 delegates and New York with 101. Of the 21 Republican contests, McCain won nine,

Romney seven and Huckabee five. But while McCain was winning big states, Romney was winning the likes of Alaska, Montana and North Dakota. He quit the race 2 days later and endorsed John McCain, having spent $118 million and won just 193 delegates. Huckabee, meanwhile, could win only in the South — Alabama, Arkansas, Georgia and Tennessee — and added the state convention in West Virginia when McCain supporters transferred *en masse* to Huckabee to stop Romney winning.

Huckabee had played a critical part in seeing off Romney by peeling away conservative votes from the former Massachusetts Governor. At the start of the race, Romney was picking up the majority of voters who thought of themselves as 'very conservative': 43% in New Hampshire and 44% in Florida. But on Super Tuesday, with Huckabee's candidacy on a roll, there is clear evidence that Huckabee's strength in such states as Georgia, Missouri and Oklahoma — and possibly California — deprived Romney of a win.

After Super Tuesday, Huckabee went on to win caucuses in Kansas and Louisiana on 9 February, suggesting that conservative Republicans were not entirely reconciled to having John McCain as their presidential candidate. But after those two defeats on 9 February, McCain swept the board in the remaining contests. Huckabee finally suspended his campaign on 4 March once McCain's victories in Ohio and Texas had confirmed him as the presumptive nominee of the Republican Party, making him only the third incumbent senator to be nominated by the Republicans in a century.

Conclusions

Why did McCain win the Republican nomination? To some extent, because other candidates imploded. Romney tried to turn himself from Michael Dukakis into Ronald Reagan in 6 months — the formerly liberal Massachusetts Governor pandering to the conservative right of the Republican Party. Giuliani adopted a bizarre strategy of sitting out the first month of the nominating contest and then crash-landed on takeoff. Fred Thompson proved utterly lacklustre, dithering for far too long before entering the race, only to discover that people were more enthused about a possible Thompson candidacy than a real one. Mike Huckabee never really broke out from being a southern candidate whose appeal did not reach far beyond the evangelical Christian wing of the party. Only Romney and Huckabee probably improved their standing within the party to the extent of being strong enough to return to the fight in 4 years' time if McCain lost in November.

In contrast to Romney and Giuliani, McCain remained true to himself. Back in 2007, he had tried to turn himself from independent maverick into establishment politician. The strategy failed and the McCain campaign spent the summer months utterly becalmed — some thought them sunk without trace. But McCain came back as the maverick that Republicans knew and respected.

Unlike Romney and Giuliani, McCain was the authentic candidate. Even when he knew he was unpopular — on the troop surge in Iraq, on immigration reform, on campaign finance reform — McCain stuck to his guns. He'd been through many harder battles in his long and eventful life.

One cannot leave the Republican nomination race without a word about Ron Paul. The Texas Republican congressman had been the Libertarian Party's presidential candidate in 1988. Other than McCain, Paul was the only candidate left standing when the primaries ended in early June. He achieved double digits in 13 states (see Table 2.3), winning 42 delegates.

Table 2.3 States in which Ron Paul gained at least 10% of the vote

State	Format of contest	Percentage of vote
Montana	Primary	25
Idaho	Primary	24
North Dakota	Caucuses	21
Maine	Caucuses	19
Alaska	Caucuses	17
South Dakota	Primary	17
Pennsylvania	Primary	16
Minnesota	Caucuses	15
Oregon	Primary	15
Nevada	Caucuses	14
New Mexico	Primary	14
Nebraska	Primary	13
Iowa	Caucuses	10

There is a clear pattern to Paul's support. First, it was often found in states that held caucuses. This shows that caucus voters tend to be more ideological than primary voters. Paul's libertarian ideology appealed to many caucus voters. Second, Paul's support came mainly from states where his brand of libertarianism is popular — rural states with a large geographic area and small population, such as Alaska, Montana and North Dakota. Geographically, the support for Paul's libertarian brand of Republicanism is found mostly in states well away from Washington DC, in the north and northwest of the United States (see Figure 2.1). His 16% showing in the Pennsylvania primary — something of a surprise — came after all the other candidates had dropped out. His anti-Iraq war rants during the Republican candidates' televised debates made him a hate figure to some but brought admiration from others. On the back of this, Paul raised a staggering $20 million in the fourth quarter of 2007 — more than Giuliani ($14 million) and McCain ($10 million). On one day alone — 16 December 2007 — he raised $6 million, believed to be a record for fundraising in a single day.

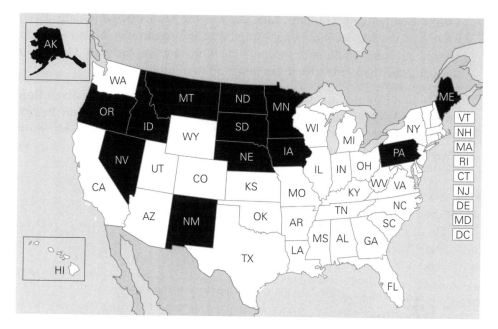

Figure 2.1 States in which Ron Paul won at least 10% of the vote (dark shading)

So the Republicans had settled on a 71-year-old senate veteran as their presidential candidate for 2008. It sounded a bit like the selection of Bob Dole in 1996. Republicans were hoping that the result would not be similar.

Questions

1 What is the 22nd Amendment and which three Republican presidents have been affected by it?
2 What were said to be John McCain's two presumed strengths?
3 What were the pros and cons of Mitt Romney and Rudy Giuliani as potential presidential candidates?
4 What decision had Giuliani made about early contests and why did this cause a problem for him?
5 Write a paragraph on how and why Mike Huckabee won the Iowa caucuses, using both data from exit polls and the comments of David Brooks in the *New York Times*.
6 What were the consequences for Huckabee of his Iowa victory?
7 Write a paragraph on how and why John McCain won the New Hampshire primary.
8 What happened in the South Carolina and Florida primaries?
9 Write a paragraph about what happened in the Republican race on Super Tuesday.
10 Why did John McCain win the Republican nomination?
11 Write a paragraph about Ron Paul's performance in the Republican primaries and caucuses.

The 2008 Democratic primaries

The candidates

As is usual for the party not currently controlling the White House, the Democrats had a large field going into the 2008 nomination race. By the close of 2007, the Democrats had eight declared candidates, as shown in Table 3.1, including four serving members of the United States Senate — Hillary Clinton of New York, Barack Obama of Illinois, Chris Dodd of Connecticut and Joe Biden of Delaware.

Table 3.1 Democratic presidential candidates

Candidate	Date entered race	Date left race
Ex-Senator Mike Gravel	17 April 2006	25 March 2008
Congressman Dennis Kucinich	11 December 2006	25 January 2008
Ex-Senator John Edwards	28 December 2006	30 January 2008
Senator Christopher Dodd	11 January 2007	3 January 2008
Senator Hillary Clinton	20 January 2007	7 June 2008
Governor Bill Richardson	21 January 2007	10 January 2008
Senator Joseph Biden	31 January 2007	3 January 2008
Senator Barack Obama	**10 February 2007**	**Eventual nominee**

As in the Republican race, it was possible to divide these would-be candidates into a first and second tier. The first-tier candidates were Senators Hillary Clinton and Barack Obama and the former North Carolina Senator and 2004 vice-presidential candidate John Edwards. Of these three, it was quite clear that Hillary Clinton was the front-runner. On 24 October 2007, with just over 2 months to go to the Iowa caucuses, Hillary Clinton (48%) had a 28 percentage-point lead over Barack Obama (20%) in nationwide polling. She had extraordinary name recognition, all the organisational and financial support of the impressive Clinton machine, front-runner status and 14 years' experience in Washington politics. Even among the first-tier candidates she was clearly the leader.

The Iowa caucuses

In spite of this, Clinton did not come first in the Iowa caucuses. When the votes were counted on the evening of 3 January 2008, Barack Obama had 38% of the vote and John Edwards 30%. Hillary Clinton was in third place with 29%. It was a devastating blow from which she never really recovered. Four years earlier John Kerry's win in Iowa had made him the front-runner in the 2004 race. The same went for Al Gore's Iowa victory in 2000. The primaries and caucuses are all about expectations, and the expectation was that Hillary Clinton would sail serenely to the nomination in 2008, not that she would be seen off by the junior Senator from Illinois. Exit polls showed Obama not only winning among male voters, but beating Clinton 35% to 30% among female voters. He won among all age groups except the over 60s, the majority of whom voted for Clinton. He won among Democrats, as well as independents and people from every income bracket.

Table 3.2 Results of the Democratic state primaries and caucuses, 2008
(winner's figures are in bold; (C) indicates caucuses)

Date	State	Obama (%)	Clinton (%)	Edwards (%)
3 January	Iowa (C)	**38**	29	30
8 January	New Hampshire	36	**39**	17
15 January	Michigan	–	**55**	–
19 January	Nevada (C)	45	**51**	4
26 January	South Carolina	**55**	26	18
29 January	Florida	33	**50**	14
5 February	Alabama	**56**	42	
	Alaska (C)	**75**	25	
	Arizona	42	**50**	
	Arkansas	26	**70**	
	California	43	**51**	
	Colorado (C)	**66**	32	
	Connecticut	**51**	47	
	Delaware	**53**	42	
	Georgia	**66**	31	
	Idaho (C)	**80**	17	
	Illinois	**65**	33	
	Kansas (C)	**74**	26	
	Massachusetts	41	**56**	
	Minnesota (C)	**66**	32	
	Missouri	**49**	48	
	New Jersey	44	**54**	
	New Mexico	48	**49**	
	New York	40	**57**	
	North Dakota (C)	**61**	37	
	Oklahoma	31	**55**	

Date	State	Obama (%)	Clinton (%)	Edwards (%)
5 February	Tennessee	40	**54**	
	Utah	**57**	39	
9 February	Louisiana	**57**	36	
	Nebraska (C)	**68**	32	
	Washington (C)	**68**	31	
10 February	Maine (C)	**60**	40	
12 February	District of Columbia	**75**	24	
	Maryland	**61**	36	
	Virginia	**64**	35	
19 February	Hawaii (C)	**76**	24	
	Wisconsin	**58**	41	
4 March	Ohio	45	**53**	
	Rhode Island	40	**58**	
	Texas	47	**51**	
	Vermont	**59**	39	
8 March	Wyoming (C)	**61**	38	
11 March	Mississippi	**61**	37	
22 April	Pennsylvania	45	**55**	
6 May	Indiana	49	**51**	
	North Carolina	**56**	42	
13 May	West Virginia	26	**67**	
20 May	Kentucky	30	**65**	
	Oregon	**59**	41	
3 June	Montana	**57**	41	
	South Dakota	45	**55**	

This was a monumental moment in American politics — one of those events like Nixon's resignation, Reagan's election or 9/11 — after which things were never going to be quite the same again. Here's how *New York Times* commentator David Brooks saw it the following day:

> Barack Obama has won the Iowa caucuses. You'd have to have a heart of stone not to feel moved by this. An African-American man wins a closely fought campaign in a pivotal state. He beats two strong opponents including the mighty Clinton machine. This is a huge moment. Iowa won't settle the race, but the rest of the primary season is going to be colored by the glow of this result.

According to Charlie Cook, writing in the *National Journal* (8 January): 'The Democratic nomination fight may not be over, but the landscape has completely changed.' And indeed, it had. The Gallup Poll of 14–16 December 2007 had Clinton on 45% and Obama on 27%. The poll taken immediately after the Iowa caucuses had them tied at 33% each.

Iowa saw the first two casualties of the race — Senators Chris Dodd and Joe Biden — both of whom pulled out immediately after miserable performances.

The New Hampshire primary

Hillary Clinton was clearly fighting for her political life. New Hampshire was the state which resurrected her husband's campaign back in 1992 and where he coined the phrase of being the 'comeback kid'. In the days between her defeat in Iowa and the voting in New Hampshire, Hillary Clinton tried to show her more personal, likeable side. So while Bill Clinton was trying to dismiss the Obama phenomenon as 'the biggest fairy tale I've ever seen', there was Hillary in a coffee shop in Portsmouth, New Hampshire, the day before voting, showing some rare human emotion. In response to a question from a sympathetic voter who wondered how she remained upbeat and 'so wonderful', Clinton's voice cracked and she choked up:

> This is very personal for me — it's not just political, it's not just public. And some people think elections are a game; they think it's like who's up and who's down. It's about our country and it's about our kids' futures — and it's really about all of us together, you know?

During 15 years in the nation's gaze, Hillary Clinton had constructed a public face that was controlled and largely inscrutable. The *Washington Post* saw this moment as 'a chink in the steely façade' of Hillary Clinton: 'The candidate, who has presented a consistent face of steely determination and invincibility, had a jarring moment of vulnerability.'

Was it this performance that tipped the scales back in her advantage when the votes were counted in the primary the next day? Just months before, Hillary Clinton had been expected to win New Hampshire comfortably. Then in the days after her third place finish in Iowa, polls showed Obama in the lead — most by quite substantial margins. So this was, in the end, a victory against the odds, but only just a victory — she had won by fewer than 8,000 votes out of over 250,000 cast (see Table 3.3). In terms of delegates, Clinton and Obama finished with nine each.

The voting in New Hampshire highlighted a huge gender gap between the two leading candidates. Whereas men voted 40–29 for Obama, women voted 46–34 for Clinton. The good news for Clinton was that 57% of New Hampshire Democratic primary voters were women while only 43% were men. Clinton beat Obama 48–32 among the over 65s, but Obama beat Clinton 60–22 among the 18–24-year-olds. Among voters earning less than $50,000, Clinton won 47–32; among voters earning more than $50,000, Obama won 40–35. Among those who had no college degree, Clinton won 43–35; among those with a college degree, Obama won 39–34. It was these socioeconomic and gender group differences that were to solidify through the next 5 months as the Democratic nomination race played out.

Table 3.3 New Hampshire Democratic primary result, 2008

Candidate	Vote	Percentage
Senator Hillary Clinton	112,251	39
Senator Barack Obama	104,772	36
Ex-Senator John Edwards	48,681	17
Governor Bill Richardson	13,249	5
Congressman Dennis Kucinich	3,919	1
Senator Joe Biden	628	0
Ex-Senator Mike Gravel	402	0
Senator Christopher Dodd	202	0
Write-in votes	2,502	1
Other candidates	716	0

More casualties ensued as Governor Bill Richardson of New Mexico bailed out following his 5% showing in New Hampshire. He would later endorse Senator Obama.

The road to Super Tuesday

The Democratic National Committee's (DNC) Rules and Bylaws Committee had ordered that only Nevada and South Carolina would be allowed to hold contests in the 4-week window between the New Hampshire primary and Super Tuesday. The two leading contenders split these between them with Clinton winning the Nevada caucuses and Obama winning the South Carolina primary. But Obama's was by far the more important win.

The Nevada caucuses attracted a mere 10,000 voters. Clinton won by just 6 percentage points in the popular vote (51–45) but Obama came away with 13 of the 25 delegates. The South Carolina primary, in contrast, attracted over half a million voters and Obama beat Clinton by a 28 percentage-point margin (55–27), walking off with 25 delegates to Clinton's 12. With 61% of the voters being women and 55% black, this was a classic battle between the two groups who stood on the threshold of getting 'one of theirs' chosen for the first time as a major party presidential candidate. So how did black women — who made up 35% of the electorate — vote? They split 78–20 for Obama. Clinton still managed to win the over-65s but in almost every other social grouping the majority voted for Obama. This was a huge boost for Obama going into Super Tuesday.

It was also a repudiation of Camp Clinton, which had mobilised Bill Clinton in South Carolina to campaign on his wife's behalf. The former president, often somewhat curiously dubbed 'the first black president', managed to offend the black community by appearing deliberately to distort some of Obama's statements for political advantage. Then, on election night, he equated Obama's win in South Carolina to Jesse Jackson's victory in the same state in 1988, which Jackson mainly achieved because other candidates had not campaigned there. Political veterans in the state said that Obama's organisation was one of the best they had seen, with some 9,000 volunteers involved in the final get-out-the-vote operation. In an article in the *Washington Post* ('Hobbled by Hubby', 29 January), commentator E. J. Dionne stated that Obama's win in South Carolina and his subsequent endorsement by Senator Ted Kennedy, 'fundamentally alters the dynamics of the 2008 Democratic presidential contest'.

The Obama camp was ecstatic with the result and in his victory speech Obama proclaimed that he was now the front-runner going into Super Tuesday:

> After four great contests, in every corner of the country, we have the most votes, the most delegates and the most diverse coalition of Americans that we've seen in a long, long time.

The crowd in Columbia, South Carolina, responded with shouts of 'Yes, we can!' and 'Race doesn't matter!' Obama now presented the race between Clinton and himself as a choice between the past and the future.

As in the Republican race, Michigan and Florida had scheduled their primaries before the date permitted by the national committee. The DNC had decided to punish the two states by stripping them of all their National Convention delegates and all candidates were asked not to campaign in either state. Obama went further and removed his name from the Michigan ballot. Thus the victories in these two states for Hillary Clinton were meaningless and gained her no delegates. This was the point at which the former North Carolina Senator John Edwards dropped out following dismal performances in New Hampshire (17%), South Carolina (18%) and Florida (14%). He would also go on to endorse Barack Obama.

Thus the scene was set for Super Tuesday, 5 February — a day when 22 states had scheduled Democratic contests, with over 1,600 delegates to be won.

Super Tuesday

Super Tuesday was a draw, with Obama just ahead on points. Of the 22 contests, Obama won 13 to Clinton's 9, but Clinton's tally included the large-population states of California, New Jersey and New York, while Obama's total included all the smaller-population states — Alaska, Colorado, Idaho, Kansas, Minnesota and North Dakota. But Obama won 8 of his 11 victories with over 60% of the vote. Clinton's victories were much narrower, except in

Arkansas — where her husband had been governor for 12 years — where she won 69% of the vote, a total she would never exceed throughout the remaining primaries. In terms of delegates won, Obama won 847 to Clinton's 834.

It was again clear from the exit polls on Super Tuesday as to who was voting for whom. Obama received the support of men, young people and first-time voters, black people, the college educated, the more wealthy and non-unionised, those who made their decision in the last month and those looking for a candidate who could 'bring about needed change'. Clinton, on the other hand, received the support of women, the elderly, white people, Hispanics, Catholics, the non-college educated, the less wealthy and the unionised, as well as voters who made their decision some time ago and who were looking for a candidate who had 'experience'.

Her lacklustre Super Tuesday performance spelt trouble ahead for Hillary Clinton. This, after all, was the day when, after victories in Iowa and New Hampshire, as well as in Michigan, Florida and South Carolina, she was to be crowned Queen of the Democratic Party in a year in which a Democrat was clearly favoured to win the White House. But there was to be no coronation for Clinton and it was Obama who clearly had the momentum as the race progressed.

Not only did Clinton lack momentum, she lacked any plan. After all, who in her team had thought that she would need a plan post-Super Tuesday? By this time she would already be the presumptive presidential nominee of her party. For the next 4 months she could sit back, maybe sip a few lattes with some up-scale voters in Rhode Island or Maryland, and watch while the Republicans fought each other in a desperate attempt to decide on a candidate. Who needed a plan?

Nine straight wins for Obama

With little momentum and no plan, Hillary Clinton floundered for the remainder of February. In contest after contest, Obama chalked up wins until he had won nine in a row in 11 days between 9 and 19 February. Most were in small, caucus-holding states like Nebraska and Hawaii. But they also included Virginia, which Obama won by 29 percentage points, and Wisconsin, which he won by 17 points. It was in these days that Hillary Clinton lost the nomination. Heading out of Super Tuesday, she was neck and neck in delegates. But in these 11 days, Obama won 288 (64%) of the 453 delegates at stake. Clinton won a mere 165 (36%), giving Obama a 123-delegate advantage. She never closed that gap.

The worst day for Clinton was the so-called Potomac Primary on 12 February, with voting in Maryland, Virginia and Washington DC. She was walloped 60–37 in Maryland, 64–35 in Virginia and 75–24 in Washington DC. Obama won 108 delegates that day to Clinton's 60. 'Is It Too Late For Hillary?' asked

Time magazine 2 days later. 'T. S. Eliot may have thought that April was the cruellest month, but as far as Hillary Clinton is concerned, it's got nothing on February,' began the *Time* magazine article. Obama's campaign manager, David Plouffe, was already stating publicly — and accurately, as it turned out — that 'we believe it's next to impossible for Senator Clinton to close the delegate count'. In contrast, Clinton sacked her campaign manager Patti Solis Doyle. Such firings usually indicate failure. The following day, 13 February, the Real Clear Politics website recorded Obama in the lead in an average of national opinion polls for the first time. In 41 days, Obama had erased a 21-point Clinton lead (see Table 3.4). She never regained it.

Table 3.4 National opinion poll average: Clinton vs Obama: 2 January – 13 February; bold type indicates candidate in the lead

Date	Clinton (%)	Obama (%)	Date	Clinton (%)	Obama (%)
2 January	**45.4**	23.8	24 January	**42.4**	33.1
3 January	**45.2**	24.0	25 January	**42.3**	33.1
4 January	**44.6**	24.4	26 January	**41.6**	33.6
5 January	**44.6**	24.2	27 January	**42.2**	32.4
6 January	**44.2**	24.2	28 January	**42.3**	32.5
7 January	**37.3**	29.3	29 January	**42.5**	32.8
8 January	**37.0**	29.3	30 January	**42.3**	33.2
9 January	**37.0**	30.0	31 January	**42.7**	34.2
10 January	**37.7**	30.7	1 February	**44.6**	36.0
11 January	**39.0**	34.0	2 February	**45.8**	36.0
12 January	**40.3**	34.7	3 February	**45.8**	40.2
13 January	**41.2**	33.8	4 February	**44.4**	41.9
14 January	**43.2**	33.4	5 February	**44.4**	41.6
15 January	**43.0**	32.6	6 February	**45.3**	41.5
16 January	**42.3**	33.3	7 February	**45.2**	41.9
17 January	**42.3**	33.4	8 February	**45.3**	42.0
18 January	**41.3**	33.1	9 February	**45.0**	41.9
19 January	**41.3**	33.2	10 February	**45.0**	41.9
20 January	**41.3**	33.4	11 February	**45.3**	43.7
21 January	**41.7**	33.2	12 February	**44.9**	43.9
22 January	**41.6**	33.6	13 February	44.3	**44.6**
23 January	**41.7**	33.3			

Source: www.realclearpolitics.com

Clinton had to spend these days dismissing Obama's wins as irrelevant and reminding anyone who would listen that 'we're going to sweep across Texas in the next 3 weeks' — a reference to the Texas primary scheduled for 4 March.

Her campaign repeated its claims that Obama was winning only small states. But that hardly explained his wins in South Carolina, Virginia, Georgia and Missouri. Further, according to the Clinton camp, Obama was winning only states with large numbers of black voters, but what about Iowa, Utah and Nebraska? Suddenly, caucuses were derided by the Clinton team as undemocratic — though, of course, this had nothing to do with the fact that Hillary Clinton had lost all but one of the 14 held thus far. The Clinton campaign wanted re-runs of the Michigan and Florida primaries, hoping no doubt that its candidate could pick up much-needed votes and delegates if they were rescheduled, but that idea got nowhere. The Clinton camp was in another world — a world away from reality, and certainly a world away from winning.

A week later — 19 February — Senator Clinton was hit hard again, this time in Wisconsin, where she lost by 17 percentage points. It was just the kind of state she should have won — 88% white with only 5% black, and over 28% blue collar workers. And yet Obama beat her even among women voters (51–49), those earning less than $50,000 (51–49), registered Democrats (50–49), married voters (53–48) and conservatives (52–48). Something symbolic happened as the two candidates were appearing in front of live television cameras after the result was declared. Senator Clinton went first and, as had become her custom of late, talked only about what she would do in Ohio and Texas in 2 weeks' time. The Obama team decided not to wait for her to finish her remarks and suddenly the television networks cut away from the Clinton wake to the Obama rally. Matt Cooper, writing in his Capital column on www.portfolio.com just hours after the result, wondered:

> Is this the last time we'll ever see a Clinton campaign? Maybe. Of course, writing off the Clintons is a famous professional hazard of journalists. But when Obama pushed her aside tonight by starting his speech while she was barely into hers, there was something poignant about it. The Clinton voice has dominated politics for so long and tonight it was pushed aside, not only by Obama's speech but by his solid victory in Wisconsin, a state that could have been hers.

'Is it panic time yet?' asked NBC. 'It's panic-button time' answered the *Associated Press* headline. According to the *New York Times*, Clinton's 'road to victory is now a cliff walk' while the *New York Observer* had her 'down to her last out'.

Hillary Clinton flew immediately to Texas to campaign for its make-or-break primary. So did Obama. He packed in a capacity crowd of more than 18,000 at the Toyota Centre in Houston, home of the National Basketball Association's Houston Rockets. But when she emerged to speak at the 6,800-seat Dodge Arena — the home of minor-league hockey team — rows upon rows of empty seats awaited. The *Washington Post's* Dana Milbank was there to cover the Clinton event:

Organizers had pulled out all the stops: a two-dozen piece mariachi band, Mexican dancers, a cowboy–cowgirl dancing act, a Goth rock band, even a guy throwing out T-shirts and shouting, 'Who's excited?' But it was no use. In the top row of the arena, Jose Bustos, wearing a Clinton T-shirt and sticker, had Section 120 to himself. 'We were expecting a little more,' he said.

For a candidate who has lost 10 contests in a row to Barack Obama and is fast becoming the Mike Huckabee of the Democratic Party, Hillary Clinton must have felt tempted to slip across the bridge near this border town and into Mexico, a fugitive from a coronation gone awry.

'Two more weeks! Two more weeks!' chanted Clinton supporters at her speech. The chant no doubt was meant as encouragement, but it also served to remind Clinton that she hasn't much time left. 'It's time to get real, to get real about how we actually win this election,' Clinton informed the crowd.

It was a brief speech, but insufficiently inspiring. After she got to the part about health care, the mariachi band headed for the exit. After she passed the part about 'alternative renewable energy' and announced her pleasure at having 'the endorsement of the United Farmworkers Union,' there was a steady flow of people from the arena floor and out the exit below Section 120. 'There's nothing wrong with America that cannot be fixed once we have new leadership,' Clinton called after them. 'I will work my heart out for you and your families.'

But who was still listening? 'Clinton Soldiers On Despite Setbacks' headlined the *Washington Post* on 23 February. The next day, the *New York Times* had added a sense of foreboding with 'Sombre Clinton Soldiers On as the Horizon Darkens'. Two days later it was 'Team Clinton: Down, and Out of Touch'. That was the evening when she was reduced to whining to the moderator in a television debate with Senator Obama:

> Well, can I just point out that in the last several debates, I seem to get the first question all the time? And if anyone saw 'Saturday Night Live', you know, maybe we should ask Barack if he's comfortable and needs another pillow.

Had it really come to this? As February ended, the Clinton campaign was pretty much out of it, and out of money. The Obama team had vastly out-raised it during both January and February. In these first 2 months of election year, Clinton had raised just over $27 million. Obama had raised $46 million. Out-raised, out-spent and out-gunned, the talk was increasingly about when she'd be … out.

Hillary's last hurrah

March and April were better months for Senator Clinton. Over a number of weeks her campaign had focused on Obama's lack of foreign experience with

an effective television ad starting with a parent looking into a child's bedroom during the night and ending with a phone ringing in the Oval Office. The commentary ran:

> It's 3 a.m. and your children are safe and asleep. But there's a phone in the White House and it's ringing. Something's happening in the world. Your vote will decide who answers that call, whether it's someone who already knows the world's leaders, knows the military, someone tested and ready to lead in a dangerous world. It's 3 a.m. and your children are safe and asleep. Who do you want answering the phone?

It was the most effective bit of campaigning by the Clinton team and it delivered results. On 4 March, Senator Clinton finally halted Obama's run of victories with wins in Ohio, Texas and Rhode Island. The win in Texas was not quite the landslide she had hoped for, and because of the curious way Texas awarded its delegates, Obama actually came out ahead with 99 delegates to her 94.

However, exit polls showed some evidence that Clinton's television ad campaign with the phone had been successful. Voters were once again seeing her as more qualified to be commander-in-chief than Senator Obama. As Table 3.5 shows, back on 12 February Democratic voters in Maryland and Virginia judged Obama was the more qualified to be commander-in-chief by 4 and 12 percentage points respectively. But on 4 March, Democratic voters in Ohio and Texas judged Clinton as more qualified by 17 and 14 percentage points respectively.

Table 3.5 Answers to the question: 'Regardless of how you voted today, which of these candidates do you think is more qualified to be commander-in-chief?'

Date/State	Obama	Clinton
12 February		
Maryland	50%	46%
Virginia	55%	43%
4 March		
Ohio	40%	57%
Texas	40%	54%

But any advantage gained at the start of the month was soon lost before the end of the month. Obama followed up with two emphatic wins — in Wyoming and Mississippi, by 23 and 24 percentage points respectively — and Hillary Clinton was on the back foot again after it was revealed that her claims to have landed in Bosnia in 1996 'under sniper fire' failed to tally with reality — or more importantly with the *CBS News* film footage of the incident. Clinton had claimed, on more than one campaign stop:

> I certainly do remember that trip to Bosnia. I remember landing under sniper fire. There was supposed to be some kind of greeting ceremony at the airport, but instead we just ran with our heads down to get into the vehicles.

The trouble was that the *CBS News* film footage showed a smiling Mrs Clinton strolling down the runway, being greeted by a little girl, and absolutely no sniper fire.

But then it was Senator Obama's turn to be on the defensive, first for remarks he made at a fundraiser in San Francisco just before the Pennsylvania primary:

> You go into these small towns in Pennsylvania, the jobs have gone now for 25 years and nothing's replaced them… So it's not surprising then that they get bitter, they cling to guns or religion or antipathy to other people who aren't like them … as a way to explain their frustrations.

The Clinton camp went after Obama for his 'bitter' remarks, portraying him as disparaging of and unfeeling for ordinary, hard-working, blue collar Americans. The remarks probably didn't go down well with the 35% of Pennsylvania Democratic primary voters who owned a gun and the similar figure who attended a religious service at least once a week. Exit polls showed both groups going heavily for Hillary Clinton.

Hardly over that spat, Obama was hit by another round of controversial remarks made by the Reverend Jeremiah Wright, the pastor of a large black church in Chicago and a personal friend of the Obamas. In a speech at the National Press Club in Washington DC at the end of April, Wright repeated his claims that America got what it deserved on 9/11 ('you cannot do terrorism on other people and expect them never to come back on you') and that the US government was guilty of 'inventing the HIV virus as a means of genocide against people of colour'. Obama had to condemn the remarks as 'divisive' and 'destructive' and went further than he had gone before in disowning both the message and the man.

Despite what had been a pretty turbulent 2 months for Obama, he was able, on 6 May, to score a huge win (56–41) in North Carolina and hold Hillary Clinton to a narrow win (51–49) in Indiana. This had really been Clinton's last chance for a comeback. If she had walloped Obama in Indiana and managed to hold him to a narrow win in North Carolina, it might just have ended differently. 'She did not get the game-changer she wanted tonight', remarked Tim Russert on MSNBC. To most independent-minded folk, this was the moment when Senator Clinton should have bowed out.

But Clinton kept going, on to the bitter end. She won nine of the last 14 primaries. She even won South Dakota on the last day, beating Obama by 10 percentage points. But it was all too little, too late. By the evening of 3 June, with super delegates moving to him in droves, Obama finally crossed the finishing line with more than the 2,118 delegates needed to clinch the nomination. In his speech that evening in Minneapolis, Obama offered a lengthy tribute to Clinton's 'barrier-breaking campaign for the presidency'. By contrast, Clinton in her speech in New York could not even bring herself to congratulate Obama on his victory, merely saying that he had run 'an extraordinary race'. It took her another 4 days to get around to admitting that he had won, that she had lost, and committing herself to supporting him wholeheartedly against John McCain in the general election campaign.

All in all, it had been the most extraordinary primary contest since the Republican race between Gerald Ford and Ronald Reagan in 1976. But unlike that one, this race turned up the result that hardly anyone expected at the start — a victory for the junior Senator from Illinois with just 3 years' experience in Washington politics. In the next chapter we address the question, 'Why did Hillary Clinton lose?'

Turnout

Before we do that, one final word about this extraordinarily protracted race for the Democratic presidential nomination. Was it good or bad for the party? Barack Obama addressed this question in his speech on the evening of the last primaries — 3 June:

> There are those who say that this primary [campaign] has somehow left us weaker and more divided. Well, I say that because of this primary campaign, there are millions of Americans who have cast their ballot for the very first time. There are Independents and Republicans who understand that this election isn't just about the party in charge in Washington, it's about the need to change Washington. There are young people, and African-Americans, and Latinos, and women of all ages who have voted in numbers that have broken all records and inspired a nation.

Table 3.6 compares the turnout in selected state primaries in 2004 with that in 2008. The average increase in turnout in these primaries was a staggering 145%. For example, the Mississippi primary on 9 March 2004 attracted just over 76,000 voters while in the same state on 11 March 2008 just under half a million voters took part, an increase of almost 500%.

When one compares this with turnout in the Republican primaries, it certainly looked like good news for Democrats. We cannot compare 2008 with 2004 for the Republicans, as that year's race was uncontested with President George W. Bush being re-nominated without a challenge.

Table 3.6 Turnout in selected Democratic primaries: 2004 and 2008 compared

State	2004 turnout	2008 turnout	Percentage change
New Hampshire	219,761	287,312	+31
South Carolina	293,843	532,227	+81
Arizona	238,942	376,458	+58
California	3,107,629	3,966,747	+28
Connecticut	130,023	352,190	+171
Delaware	33,291	96,341	+189
Georgia	626,738	1,049,174	+67
Louisiana	161,653	384,348	+138
Maryland	481,476	777,675	+62
Massachusetts	614,296	1,216,154	+98
Missouri	418,339	823,503	+97
New York	715,633	1,745,791	+144
Oklahoma	302,385	417,569	+38
Tennessee	369,385	617,397	+67
Utah	34,854	124,307	+257
Wisconsin	826,250	1,110,702	+34
Ohio	1,221,014	2,224,907	+82
Rhode Island	35,759	186,339	+421
Texas	839,231	2,911,036	+247
Vermont	82,881	154,653	+87
Mississippi	76,298	454,110	+495
Pennsylvania	787,034	2,306,664	+193
Indiana	317,211	1,274,993	+302
Montana	93,543	181,423	+94

In Table 3.7, however, we can compare turnout in Republican primaries in 2008 with turnout in 2000, the last time there was a contested Republican presidential race. What the table shows is a very mixed picture, with turnout up modestly in some states such as Delaware and North Carolina but actually down in 10 states including Michigan, Ohio and California. Overall, compared with 2000, turnout in these 22 selected states was up just 7% on average. Political commentator Mort Kondracke referred to what he called 'a vast enthusiasm gap between the two parties.'

Table 3.7 Turnout in selected Republican primaries: 2000 and 2008 compared

State	2000 turnout	2008 turnout	Percentage change
New Hampshire	238,206	238,328	+1
Michigan	1,276,770	868,083	−32
South Carolina	573,101	443,203	−23
Arizona	322,669	451,584	+40
California	2,847,921	2,251,236	−21
Connecticut	178,985	151,119	−16
Delaware	30,060	50,237	+67
Georgia	643,188	958,399	+49
Maryland	376,034	291,217	−23
Missouri	475,363	589,289	+24
New York	720,000	605,529	−16
Wisconsin	495,769	409,078	−17
Ohio	1,397,528	1,062,276	−24
Rhode Island	36,120	26,996	−25
Texas	1,126,757	1,384,663	+23
Vermont	81,355	39,490	−51
Mississippi	114,979	143,286	+25
Pennsylvania	643,085	807,123	+26
Indiana	406,664	411,948	+1
North Carolina	322,517	522,635	+62
South Dakota	45,279	60,791	+34
New Mexico	75,230	108,993	+45

Clearly Democratic voters were more energised than Republican voters. But were they more divided? Back in 1976, Democratic Congressman Morris Udall of Arizona, who lost almost every primary to the eventual nominee Jimmy Carter, claimed to have come across a prayer for Democratic primaries. It went like this: 'O Lord, may I utter words that are tender and sweet, because some day I may have to eat them.' It was a prayer that did not often appear to be on the lips of the junior Senator from New York, Hillary Rodham Clinton.

Questions

1 Write a paragraph about the result of the Iowa caucuses.
2 What did David Brooks mean by stating that 'the rest of the primary season is going to be colored by the glow of this result'?
3 What immediate effect did Obama's win in Iowa have on the poll numbers of Obama and Clinton?
4 Write a paragraph about the result of the New Hampshire primary.
5 Why was the result of the South Carolina primary so significant?
6 Analyse what happened in the Democratic race on Super Tuesday.
7 What happened in the Democratic race during the remainder of February? Explain why Hillary Clinton had no plan for this period in the race.
8 What message was Hillary Clinton trying to convey by her television ad about a 3 a.m. phone call at the White House? How effective was the ad?
9 How did Hillary Clinton get into difficulties over reminiscing about a trip to Bosnia in 1996?
10 How did Barack Obama get into difficulties over a speech in San Francisco?
11 Who was Jeremiah Wright and how did he cause problems for Barack Obama?
12 Compare and contrast the turnout in the Democratic and Republican primaries.

Chapter 4

Why did Hillary Clinton lose the Democratic nomination?

'I'm in it for the long run. It's not a very long run. It'll be over by February 5.' So said Hillary Clinton in a television interview on ABC's *This Week* on 30 December 2007, just 4 days before voting in the Iowa caucuses. That's how confident she was. Back in 2007, when top aides and advisers on Clinton's team were asked if she could win the presidency, they had their answer ready: 'She's already winning.' That was how confident her top aides like chief strategist Mark Penn and campaign chairman Terry McAuliffe were of Clinton's ability not just to win the Democratic Party's nomination, but to win the White House.

This was supposed to be a coronation, not a competition. This year was supposed to see the first woman selected as a major party's presidential candidate, not an African-American. It was supposed to be all about 'experience', not 'change'. This, we were told, was Hillary Clinton's year. She had been planning for it for a decade or more. When she ran for a senate seat from New York in 2000, everyone knew it was just a staging post to the Oval Office. Even as the Clintons left the White House in January 2001, Hillary had turned to some of the domestic staff and promised, 'We'll be back!' 'What hurt them was their sense of entitlement that the presidency was theirs', said Governor Bill Richardson of New Mexico, a one-time member of Bill Clinton's cabinet, who was dubbed 'a Judas' by Clinton cheerleader James Carville when he endorsed Barack Obama.

When Hillary Clinton was entering the United States Senate in early January 2001, Barack Obama was still just a member of the Illinois state senate. In 2004, the Democrats had nominated John Kerry as their presidential candidate, someone who had been in the US Senate for 20 years. In 2000, it had nominated Al Gore — a member of Congress for 16 years and vice-president for eight. Surely the Democrats would not nominate someone who just 4 years earlier was a state legislator? But that's precisely what they did. As well as telling the story of this remarkable political turnaround, we must also answer the question: 'Why did Hillary Clinton lose the 2008 presidential nomination for the Democratic Party?'

In covering the narrative of the Obama–Clinton race in Chapter 3, we have alluded to a number of reasons why it ended as it did. In modern US political history no establishment candidate with so many seeming advantages has failed to secure the presidential nomination of their party. She had enormous name recognition, the best brand name in Democratic Party politics, money to burn, a commanding lead in the opinion polls, a seemingly invincible organisation, experience, and a husband who was thought of as one of the greatest campaigners in twentieth-century American politics. In this chapter, we shall consider six reasons why Hillary Clinton lost the race she was expected to win so comfortably.

Poor organisation, personnel and management

It is ironic that such a personally disciplined politician as Hillary Clinton ran such a disorganised and ill-disciplined campaign team. But it was a campaign modelled on how things were — back in 1992 when Bill Clinton had first run for the White House. It had significant personnel weaknesses — campaign manager Patti Solis Doyle and chief strategist Mark Penn being the two whom most people blamed for the organisational failures.

Solis Doyle had been on Mrs Clinton's staff for 17 years, eventually becoming the First Lady's scheduler. However, she had absolutely no experience that equipped her to lead what would become a $200 million presidential campaign with nearly 1,000 employees. Having finished third in Iowa, Clinton decided she needed a new campaign manager and told Solis Doyle this, but other staff members protested. Clinton made a fatal hesitation and Solis Doyle stayed on for over a month. By the time she was removed in mid-February, the nomination was already almost out of Clinton's reach. The *Wall Street Journal* reported in early June 2008 that Solis Doyle still had a Hillary Clinton sign up in the garden of her Washington DC home, but that she and Clinton had not spoken since her removal 4 months earlier. 'I take my fair share of the responsibility for the mistakes that were made,' Solis Doyle told the newspaper.

In the Clinton campaign team there was no clear chain of command or accountability. The team often confused discipline with insularity. This is how people on the Clinton campaign staff saw it:

> Campaign manager Patti Solis Doyle and her deputy Mike Henry sat up there in their offices and no-one knew what they did all day. Patti's a nice person who was put in a job way over her head. She was out of her element... Nobody was truly in charge, nobody held truly accountable... The headquarters' most senior staff had no real presidential campaign experience, and no primary experience whatsoever. Notoriously bad managers, they filled key posts with newcomers loyal to them but unknown to and unfamiliar with the candidate, her style, her history, her preferences.

Many on Clinton's staff had been critical right from the start that Mark Penn — another long-time Clinton crony — was the campaign's only pollster. Most campaigns would use a number of pollsters: at this point Senator Obama had four. Solis Doyle says that throughout 2006 and 2007, she urged Senator

Clinton to add more. But Clinton claimed that this was unnecessary because Mark Penn was 'brilliant'. Recruiting Mark Penn at all was probably another fatal mistake of the former First Lady. Penn had run Bill Clinton's successful re-election campaign in 1996. But at that time, Mr Clinton was the incumbent president and the opposition — Republican Bob Dole — was not exactly sparkling. Furthermore, Penn seemed blithely unaware that the conduct and financing of elections had changed dramatically during the intervening 12 years. Penn didn't even give up his other full-time job as CEO of a huge public relations firm, Burson-Masteller Worldwide. When it was revealed in April that in that capacity, Penn had been lobbying for a Colombian trade pact that Mrs Clinton opposed, Penn was replaced at the Clinton campaign, though he remained in frequent touch with both Clintons. According to Rick Klein:

> Staff-infighting — often with Penn at the centre of the controversy — left the campaign virtually paralysed at critical junctures, with major strategic changes coming too late to make a major difference.
>
> Source: 'What Went Wrong? How Hillary Lost', 3 June 2008. www.abcnews.go.com

Even as she flew from one town hall meeting to another, from rally to rally and from coast to coast, 'she did little to stop the infighting back home among advisers who nursed grudges from their White House days', concludes Peter Baker ('The Long Road to Exit', *New York Times*, 8 June 2008). Clinton's staff were 'distracted from battling Senator Obama while they hurled expletives at one another, stormed out of meetings and schemed to get one another fired'.

Poor organisation and management was also reflected in the Clinton campaign's failure to beat Obama in the money primary. As *The Economist* (7 June 2008) commented: 'Mrs Clinton built the best fund-raising machine of the 20th century, but Mr Obama trumped her by building the best fund-raising machine of the 21st century.' The Clinton campaign was still raising money the old way, through 'fat cats' and 'whales' — big money donors who wrote cheques for four-figure sums. They tended to give only once. Team Obama, on the other hand, was raising its money through the internet, using its campaign website like a social networking site. Obama's supporters gave $100, $50 or less, but they gave again and again. By giving, they became part of the huge network of Obama supporters from every state, from every congressional district, from every county across America.

In the first 3 months of 2008, Obama raised more money than Clinton on 81 out of 91 days. Five days after his huge win in the South Carolina primary, Obama raised just short of $4 million in one day — 31 January. On 6 February — the day after Super Tuesday — Obama raised another $3 million. Clinton raised only $250,000 that day. In the same 3 months, Obama raised over $63 million to Clinton's $34 million. He was out-raising her almost 2:1.

Change, not experience

Back in 2007, as the Democratic race was shaping up, most commentators had presumed that American voters would be looking for experience in the Oval Office in January 2009. This is not always the case. Indeed, it might be possible to justify the claim that in previous presidential elections, the American voter had elected the *least* experienced candidate in the November election. President George H. W. Bush (1992) and Vice-President Al Gore (2000) both offered more political experience than Bill Clinton (1992) and George W. Bush (2000). But it was presumed that with America at war in Iraq and Afghanistan and with the continuing 'war on terror', the 2008 election would be about experience. 'She made an initial strategic blunder by focusing on experience in a Democratic primary,' said Dick Morris, who once advised President Bill Clinton but became a critic of Senator Hillary Clinton. 'They don't want experience. They want change and newness. That's why they're Democrats.'

Clinton had made a fatal mistake even before the race had started. Before the January 2007 announcement of her candidacy, her team argued over how the former First Lady should portray herself to voters. The majority of her senior staff, including Patti Solis Doyle, wanted to promote her as a candidate of change — the first woman president. They also realised that many people regarded Hillary as somewhat imperious, remote and cold. They wanted to present her warmer, more personal side. But Mark Penn believed that Clinton had to be the steely chief executive, capable of being commander-in-chief. Emphasising her gender too much, he argued, would undercut that. Clinton took Penn's advice.

> Running as an incumbent, as the inevitable candidate, was probably our biggest mistake, particularly in a time when the country was really hungry for change.

That was how one Clinton staffer summed it up at the end. In one exit poll after another, Democratic primary voters said that they wanted a candidate who 'can bring about needed change' rather than one who 'has the right experience'. As Table 4.1 shows, 'change' scored over 'experience' in every exit poll by anything from 17 (Texas) to 45 (Georgia) percentage points.

Among those voters who said that change was their most important determining quality, Obama won by huge margins in every state bar West Virginia. In Georgia, among the 62% of voters who said that 'bringing about needed change' was the most important quality in deciding how they voted, 83% voted for Obama and just 16% for Clinton. On the other hand, among those voters who said that experience was their most important determining quality, Clinton won by a margin of anything from 44 (Iowa) to 93 (Kentucky) percentage points. The trouble for Clinton, however, was that no more than 28% of voters fell into this category in any state primary or caucus.

Table 4.1 Voters' responses in selected primaries to the question:
'Which quality mattered most in deciding how you voted today?'

State	*Change (%)	Obama (%)	Clinton (%)	†Experience (%)	Obama (%)	Clinton (%)
Iowa	52	51	19	20	5	49
New Hampshire	54	55	28	19	5	71
South Carolina	54	75	15	14	7	84
California	49	64	33	23	6	89
Georgia	62	83	16	17	8	90
Illinois	63	82	16	16	9	87
Missouri	53	64	33	20	4	93
New Jersey	52	64	35	26	3	94
New York	50	62	36	26	2	97
Virginia	56	82	17	21	6	93
Wisconsin	52	77	20	24	5	95
Ohio	47	73	27	28	6	94
Texas	44	72	27	27	8	91
Indiana	49	70	30	23	3	96
North Carolina	50	77	21	22	10	85
West Virginia	47	44	50	23	2	91
Kentucky	46	54	44	22	1	94
Montana	57	82	16	20	7	91
South Dakota	50	66	34	22	7	93

* Can bring about needed change   † Has the right experience

Once the race had been framed as one about 'change', it was exceedingly difficult for Clinton to come out in front. How could a 60-year-old who had been in Washington for 16 years claim that she was the candidate of 'change' as opposed to the 46-year-old who had arrived in Washington just 3 years earlier? To present a presidential succession of Bush–Clinton–Bush–Clinton in terms of 'change' would have been a tall order for any politician.

The Iowa defeat

Hillary Clinton's third-place finish in Iowa was a huge setback and from the evening of 3 January she was always on the defensive. According to a Clinton campaign staffer: 'It was obvious talking to people on the ground there that they simply didn't get the Iowa caucus from a field perspective. That's where the thing was lost.' Coming back from a second-place finish in Iowa is doable, provided that it is followed by a strong showing in following contests, particularly New Hampshire. In 1988, the eventual presidential nominees of both parties — Democrat Michael Dukakis and Republican George Bush — finished third in Iowa, but both rebounded strongly afterwards. Dukakis won the New Hampshire primary by 16 percentage points while Bush won New Hampshire by a modest 9 percentage points but went on to win 16 out the 17 Super Tuesday contests.

The only other eventual nominee not to win Iowa in recent elections was Republican Ronald Reagan in 1980. He finished second — losing by just 2 points to George H. W. Bush. But he went on to beat Bush by 27 percentage points in New Hampshire. Hillary Clinton not only came in third in Iowa but barely eked out a win in New Hampshire, lost heavily in South Carolina and could only 'draw' with Obama on Super Tuesday.

No plan past Super Tuesday

Clinton had presented her candidacy as 'inevitable': she expected a coronation. Therefore the fourth reason why she failed was that the Clinton campaign had no plan past Super Tuesday on 5 February. 'It'll be over by February 5', she had claimed. Thus Clinton was defeated by her own hubris, and in the weeks after Super Tuesday she was hammered in defeat after defeat. Up to and through Super Tuesday (3 January to 5 February), Obama and Clinton were neck and neck. The same was true from March to June. But in those vital last 3 weeks in February, Obama picked up 288 pledged delegates to Clinton's 165, a lead of 123. It was a lead she never erased. 'There was not any plan in place from beginning to end on how to win the nomination', commented a member of Clinton's campaign staff. Obama did have such a plan and it showed.

The lack of any coherent plan showed as the Clinton campaign lurched from one tactic to another with little obvious continuity. One day she was telling Obama, 'Shame on you!' and the next she was saying how 'honoured' she was to be sharing a platform with him. One day she was saying how inexperienced and unsuitable for the presidency he was; the next she claimed he might be her vice-presidential running-mate.

Clinton was so confident of sweeping Super Tuesday and the big states which followed, such as Ohio, Pennsylvania and Texas, that the Clinton team regarded caucus states as irrelevant. Except for Iowa — where it lost — Team Clinton was nowhere to be seen in the caucus states. This error of judgement gave Obama another vital advantage. As Table 4.2 shows, Obama won 12 of the 13 caucus states and even when he lost in Nevada, he still managed to gain three more delegates than Clinton. In total, Obama amassed 283 delegates in caucus states to Clinton's 142 — a lead of 141 delegates. By the end of the primary and caucus season, Obama had a lead in pledged delegates of just 127. Clinton's failure to compete in the caucus states was another significant strategic error.

Table 4.2 Results of Democratic caucuses and delegates won

State	Winner of caucus	Obama delegates	Clinton delegates
Iowa	Obama	25	14
Nevada	Clinton	14	11
Alaska	Obama	10	3
Colorado	Obama	36	19
Idaho	Obama	15	3
Kansas	Obama	23	9
Minnesota	Obama	48	24
North Dakota	Obama	8	5
Nebraska	Obama	16	8
Washington	Obama	52	26
Maine	Obama	15	9
Hawaii	Obama	14	6
Wyoming	Obama	7	5
Total number of delegates won		283	142

Bill Clinton

> Bill's behaviour that started off in Iowa, carried on in New Hampshire, and culminated in South Carolina really was the beginning of the end. Unfortunately, for whatever reason, he just kind of imploded. I think, if I had to look back on it, it became more about him than about her. It really was destructive overall.

Again, this is not the assessment of the unsympathetic media, of which both the Clintons so frequently complained during these months. This is the assessment of one of Clinton's own campaign staff.

With his 'fairy tale' comment, his allegation that Obama was 'playing the race card' against him, and his frequent red-faced tantrums, Bill Clinton switched from senior statesman to Mr Punch in a matter of a few weeks. The former president was even given a public reproof by South Carolina Representative Jim Clyburn, the highest-ranking African-American in Congress, when he told Bill Clinton to 'chill a little bit'. On the night of the South Carolina primary Mr Clinton called Mr Clyburn and they spoke by telephone for 50 minutes. 'Let's just say it wasn't pleasant,' Mr Clyburn stated. Democrats familiar with the exchange claim that Mr Clinton called Mr Clyburn an expletive. Mr Clyburn's office would confirm only that the former president used 'offensive words'. It was widely reported that Bill Clinton's outbursts were one factor that pushed Senator Ted Kennedy into making such an early endorsement of Barack Obama.

It is also possible partly to attribute Hillary Clinton's drubbing in South Carolina to her husband's racial slurs and public outbursts. 'She was moving,' said one Clinton veteran, 'and then *he* got in the way.' When exit polls asked South Carolina Democratic primary voters, 'In your vote in today's primary, how would you rate the importance of Bill Clinton campaigning?', among the 58% who said it was 'important' Obama had an 11 percentage-point lead over Clinton.

The press certainly jumped on the former president. In early February, *Newsweek* ran a 6-page story headlined: 'Just Don't Know What to Do With Myself: Bill Clinton has morphed from statesman into attack dog.' Less kindly, the tabloid *New York Post* carried a picture of the two Clintons under the headline 'The Two-Headed Monster'. The broadsheet *New York Times* was no kinder, with commentator Maureen Dowd claiming that 'Bill's transition from elder statesman, leader of his party and bipartisan ambassador to hatchet man has been seamless — and seamy'. It seemed ironic that in trying to become the first female presidential candidate of a major party, and the first woman president, Hillary Clinton was seeming to have to rely on her husband to do her dirty work for her. According to a Clinton team insider: 'The issue became, "if she can't control her husband in the campaign, who the hell is really going to run this White House?"'

The party rules and calendar

Ironically, Hillary Clinton was scuppered as much by her party's rules and the calendar of state primaries as by anything else. Terry McAuliffe and Harold Ickes, two of Clinton's top advisers, knew more about the Democrats' delegate selection process than virtually anyone in America. But you would never have known it from the Clinton campaign plan.

'Clinton's Fate Was Sealed by the Calendar,' was the headline in the *New York Observer* (23 May). 'It was the calendar that killed Hillary Clinton's 2008 presidential campaign,' the article concluded. If only Florida and Michigan had held their primaries a few weeks later. If only Texas, Ohio, West Virginia or Kentucky had moved their primaries up to mid-February, giving her a chance to follow up Super Tuesday with some big wins. Instead, they came far too late to be anything more than token victories, winning battles after the war had been lost. As the *New York Observer* rightly concluded:

> Clinton didn't lose simply because she didn't organise in Louisiana and Nebraska and all the other mid-February states. She was in trouble as soon as they were placed on the calendar.

If only the Democrats had allowed states to have winner-takes-all primaries. If just California and New York had winner-takes-all contests — as they do in their Republican primaries — Clinton would have added an extra 259 delegates and she would have been the nominee.

Then there was the Florida and Michigan fiasco. As we saw in Chapter 3, these two states scheduled their primaries ahead of the date allowed by the rules laid down by the Democratic National Committee (DNC). The DNC stripped both states of all their convention delegates, making their primaries — which Hillary Clinton might reasonably have expected to win — meaningless. Clinton loyalists, including DNC member Harold Ickes, had initially supported the decision to punish both states by removing their delegates. But in the final weeks of the campaign, Ickes and others on Clinton's team spent huge amounts of time arguing that the delegates from both states should be allowed into the convention after all. In the end, the DNC compromised, allowing delegates from both states to attend the convention but with only half a vote each. Yet, as Rick Klein of ABC News commented: 'If Michigan and Florida had counted from the start, the race would have looked very different — in delegates, in the popular vote, and in the intangible quality of early momentum.'

Conclusion

Hillary Clinton spent a year as her party's prohibitive front-runner, and then 5 months reeling from forces and circumstances that she and her advisers could not, or did not, see coming. In the end, race trumped gender. Black women voted in overwhelming numbers for Obama, especially after he had won in predominantly-white Iowa. Clinton soon discovered that she was up against not a person so much as a phenomenon. Wherever he went, Obama drew huge, cheering, banner-waving, cell-phone photo-snapping, swooning supporters. Clinton's crowds were smaller, quieter, more polite.

Looking back on the race, the Clinton campaign suffered from structural defects before it even started. As Peter Baker concluded in the *New York Times* ('The Long Road to a Clinton Exit', 8 June 2008) when it was all over:

> While she emphasised its trailblazing nature as she exited the race, her campaign also represented a back-to-the-future effort to restore the Democratic dynasty of the 1990s that could never quite escape the past. Although Mrs Clinton proved a more agile candidate than many had expected, she built a campaign that was suffused in overconfidence, riven with acrimony and weighed down by the emotional baggage of a marriage between former and would-be presidents.

The Clintons found that Barack Obama was singing the same message of change and hope that they had sung back in 1992. Back then, Bill Clinton proclaimed he was a 'New Democrat', but there was precious little that was new about the Clintons 16 years later.

Questions

1 Give some examples of Hillary Clinton's over-confidence that she would win in 2008.
2 In what ways was Hillary Clinton's campaign poorly organised and poorly managed?
3 Compare the fundraising techniques of Hillary Clinton and Barack Obama.
4 Explain why voters' desire for 'change' rather than 'experience' contributed to Hillary Clinton's defeat.
5 How had candidates in previous election cycles managed to win their party's nomination after losing in Iowa? Why did Hillary Clinton not recover from her loss in Iowa?
6 How did Hillary Clinton's lack of a plan past Super Tuesday contribute to her defeat?
7 How and to what extent did Bill Clinton become a drag on the campaign rather than an asset?
8 How did the Democratic Party rules and calendar contribute to Hillary Clinton's defeat?

Chapter 5

The conventions: running-mates, delegates and 'bounce'

What you need to know

- National Party Conventions meet for about 4 days during the late summer of the presidential election year.
- By tradition, the 'challenging party' — the Democrats in 2008 — holds its convention first.
- The conventions are attended by the delegates, who are mostly chosen during the primaries and caucuses.
- The conventions are said to have three main functions: choosing the party's presidential candidate; choosing the party's vice-presidential candidate; deciding on the party platform, i.e. the manifesto.
- But nowadays all three functions are done before the conventions meet.
- The significance of modern-day conventions is therefore questionable.

Obama's choice of running-mate

At around 3 a.m. on the morning of Saturday 23 August 2008, thousands of people across America received a text message from Barack Obama on their mobile phones. It read: 'Barack has chosen Senator Joe Biden to be our VP nominee. Watch the first Obama-Biden rally live at 3 p.m. on **www.BarackObama.com**. Spread the word!' It was the first time that a presidential candidate had announced his vice-presidential selection electronically. This was just 2 days before the start of the Democratic National Convention.

Senator Joe Biden was first elected to the US Senate from the state of Delaware in 1972 at the age of 30 — the minimum age required to be a senator. At the time he was the fifth-youngest senator in US history. It was a narrow victory by less than 4,000 votes in over 228,000 cast. Biden has been re-elected six times since, and in 2008 was up for re-election to his seventh term. He decided to run for both offices, which is permitted by Delaware state law.

In his personal life, Biden has had some significant brushes with tragedy. Just 6 weeks after his 1972 Senate win, his wife and 1-year-old daughter were killed in a car crash while out Christmas shopping. His two sons were critically injured but both made full recoveries. Biden considered resigning from the Senate to care for his two sons but was persuaded not to. Instead he commuted on the train from Washington DC to Wilmington, Delaware, every day. Five years later, Biden married his present wife Jill, who like him is a devout Roman Catholic.

In the Senate, Biden is known for his lengthy speeches. While running for the presidential nomination of his party in 2008, Biden was taking part in a debate with his fellow Democratic hopefuls. NBC anchor Brian Williams was asking the questions and quoted to Biden a *Los Angeles Times* editorial that said, 'In addition to his uncontrolled verbosity, Biden is a gaffe machine.' Williams then asked Biden, 'Can you reassure voters in this country that you would have the discipline you would need on the world stage, Senator?' Biden responded with what might have been the first one-word answer of his entire political career: 'Yes', prompting gales of laughter from the audience.

Biden has made two unsuccessful bids for the presidential nomination. The first, in 1988, ended under somewhat bizarre circumstances when he was revealed to have plagiarised parts of a speech made by the then British Labour Party leader, Neil Kinnock. During the 1987 UK general election, Kinnock had included in one of his party election broadcasts a clip of a speech with him saying:

> Why am I the first Kinnock in a thousand generations to be able to get to university? Why is [my wife] Glenys the first woman in her family in a thousand generations to be able to get to university? Was it because all our predecessors were thick?

The following year, a speech by presidential candidate Joe Biden included the lines:

> I started thinking as I was coming over here, why is it that Joe Biden is the first in his family ever to go to a university? Why is it that my wife is the first in her family to ever go to college? Is it because our fathers and mothers were not bright? Is it because I'm the first Biden in a thousand generations to get to college and a graduate degree that I was smarter than the rest?

The campaign staff of Biden's chief Democratic rival, Governor Michael Dukakis of Massachusetts, made a video by cutting and pasting the Kinnock and Biden speeches against each other and sent it to a number of major US news organisations. Biden withdrew from the race.

In 2008, 20 years after his previous bid, Biden made another bid for his party's presidential nomination. But having finished in fifth place in the Iowa caucuses, gaining less than 1% of the votes, Biden withdrew.

In the Senate, Biden made his name with two high profile committee assignments. He was a member of the powerful Senate Judiciary Committee and served as chairman of the committee between January 1987 and January 1995. He was therefore chairing the committee during the controversial inquiries into the Supreme Court nominations by President Ronald Reagan of Robert Bork in 1987 and by President George H. W. Bush of Clarence Thomas in 1991. More recently, Biden served as chairman of the Senate Foreign Relations Committee, another of the most prestigious standing committees of the US Senate.

As Table 5.1 shows, Biden comes from a distinguished line of Democratic Senators who became their party's vice-presidential nominee — Harry Truman, Lyndon Johnson, Hubert Humphrey, Walter Mondale and Al Gore, to name but five. Indeed, since 1944, 14 of the 15 initial vice-presidential nominees of the Democratic Party have been serving Senators; Geraldine Ferraro, a serving member of the House of Representatives, is the only exception.

Table 5.1 Previous political office held by Democratic vice-presidential candidates, 1944–2008

Year	Democratic vice-presidential candidate	Political office held
1944	Harry Truman	Senator
1948	Alben Barkley	Senator
1952	John Sparkman	Senator
1956	Estes Kefauver	Senator
1960	Lyndon Johnson	Senator
1964	Hubert Humphrey	Senator
1968	Ed Muskie	Senator
1972	†Thomas Eagleton	Senator
1972	Sargent Shriver	Former US Ambassador
1976/1980	Walter Mondale	Senator
1984	Geraldine Ferraro	Representative
1988	Lloyd Bentsen	Senator
1992/1996	Al Gore	Senator
2000	Joe Lieberman	Senator
2004	John Edwards	Senator
2008	Joe Biden	Senator

† Thomas Eagleton withdrew from the ticket and was replaced by Sargent Shriver

Obama's choice of Biden was seen as being in the same mould as George W. Bush's choice of Dick Cheney in 2000. Obama, with little Washington experience, needed someone to bring gravitas and experience to the ticket, especially in foreign policy. The chairman of the Senate Foreign Relations Committee with 36 years of Washington experience fitted the bill very well. It was the first time two incumbent senators had run together on a presidential ticket since John Kennedy and Lyndon Johnson in 1960.

The Democratic Convention

The Democrats held their convention in Denver, Colorado — the first time in the Mile High city for exactly 100 years. The last time they were there, in 1908, they took 46 ballots to nominate William Jennings Bryan, who went on to lose in a landslide to the Republicans' William Howard Taft. The omens, therefore, weren't good. But there weren't 46 ballots to nominate Barack Obama. Indeed, although the Obama team had agreed to there being a traditional roll-call of the states for the presidential nomination it was cut short when, at 4.47 p.m. (Mountain Time) on the Wednesday afternoon of the convention, Senator Clinton took the microphone on the convention floor and asked the Convention Chair, House Speaker Nancy Pelosi, to suspend the roll-call and declare Senator Obama the presidential nominee by acclamation. As the *New York Times* reported, 'that it did with a succession of loud roars, followed by a swirl of dancing, embracing, high-fiving and chants of "Yes, we can".' It was perfect timing, coming right in the middle of the early evening news broadcasts on the east coast. Before that acclamation, Obama had gained 3188.5 votes and Clinton 1010.5 votes in the delegate roll-call.

Earlier, Michelle Obama had taken to the podium on the Monday night to give her personal story of her husband. But Mrs Obama's speech was somewhat eclipsed by an unscheduled appearance by the ailing veteran Senator Ted Kennedy, who had only weeks before undergone surgery for a brain tumour.

Tuesday night featured a rousing speech from Hillary Clinton in which she seemed to wholeheartedly endorse Barack Obama. 'Were you in this campaign just for me?' she asked her supporters. One worried that, given half a chance, the shout of 'yes' might have been heard from the Clinton delegates. 'Or were you in it for all the people in this country who feel invisible?' Forget all the bickering of the primaries, Barack Obama was now her candidate, 'and he must be our president,' she declared.

On Wednesday, it was the turn of former president Bill Clinton to wow the crowds. 'Last night Hillary told us in no uncertain terms that she is going to do everything she can to elect Barack Obama: that makes two of us!' he proclaimed to wild applause. He even reminded the delegates of how opponents had written him off when he first ran for the presidency in 1992: 'The Republicans said I was too young and too inexperienced to be commander-in-chief. Sound familiar?'

Wednesday also saw vice-presidential nominee Joe Biden deliver his acceptance speech. It was not vintage stuff. Biden tends to like listening to himself more than his audience does. But he did manage a reasonable quip at Vice-President Cheney's expense, when he promised that under an Obama–Biden administration 'the eight most dreaded words in English will no longer be "The vice-president's office is on the phone"'.

For the final night, the convention decamped from the Pepsi Center in downtown Denver to INVESCO Field, the home of the Denver Broncos. This was the first time in nearly 50 years that a party had held an open session of its convention — the last time being the Democratic Convention of 1960. A capacity crowd of nearly 85,000 packed the stadium and a viewing audience of an estimated 38 million Americans watched the speech delivered by Barack Obama on the 10 cable and terrestrial television channels that covered it live. It was the most extraordinary event — part pop concert, part political rally.

Poignantly, Obama's speech was delivered 45 years to the day after Martin Luther King had delivered his 'I Have a Dream' speech in Washington DC. Obama's speech was measured in tone but not hugely memorable in content. He was cheered when he talked of the 'failed presidency of George W. Bush' and 'the broken politics in Washington'. 'America, we are better than these last eight years; we are a better country than this,' he declared. And he described his Republican rival as out of touch with ordinary voters, saying: 'It's not because John McCain doesn't care, it's because John McCain doesn't get it.' He spoke about some of the steps he, Obama, would take if elected president — tax cuts for the middle class; weaning the country from dependence on Middle Eastern oil. On foreign policy, Obama criticised President Bush for failing, in his eyes, to match tough talk with tough action:

> You don't defeat a terrorist network that operates in 80 countries by occupying Iraq. You don't protect Israel and deter Iran by talking tough in Washington.

Obama delivered much the same judgement on John McCain:

> John McCain likes to say that he'll follow Osama bin Laden to the gates of hell, but he won't even follow him to the cave where he lives.

The end of the Obama speech was followed by a spectacular firework display instead of the usual indoor balloons and confetti. When all was said and done, the convention had achieved its primary aim — party unity. Delegates left Denver believing that they had a winning team in Barack Obama and Joe Biden.

The Democratic delegates

In the end there were 4,400 delegates at the Democratic Convention, of which around 81% were chosen through the primaries and caucuses as pledged delegates, with the remaining 19% being unpledged — commonly known as super delegates. Just as voters in the party primaries and caucuses tend to be unrepresentative of general election voters — they tend to be more ideological — so delegates to the National Conventions are also somewhat unrepresentative.

Table 5.2 Selected policy positions and personal characteristics of Democratic National Convention delegates, 2008

Characteristic	All voters (%)	Democrat voters (%)	Democrat delegates (%)
US should have stayed out of Iraq	59	84	95
Abortion should be permitted in all cases	26	33	58
Abortion should be generally available to those who want it	33	43	70
Gay couples should be allowed to legally marry	34	49	55
Member of a labour union	10	10	24
Describe yourself as an evangelical Christian	27	23	14
Describe yourself as 'very liberal'	8	15	19
Describe yourself as 'very conservative'	15	6	1
White	83	72	65
Post-graduate educated	12	13	55
Earn over $75,000 per year	31	26	70
Female	54	58	49
National Party Conventions are still needed	56	66	88

Source: *New York Times*, 25 August 2008

As Table 5.2 shows, delegates to this year's Democratic Convention were more anti-war, pro-choice and pro-gay marriage than even typical Democratic voters, let alone voters in general. They were far more likely to be a member of a labour union, less likely to be an evangelical Christian, more likely to be liberal, less likely to be white, and were more educated and wealthier than typical Democratic voters. They also had a much more positive view of National Party Conventions. But does this all matter?

It certainly does matter when convention delegates — who are given the task of signing off on the Party Platform — are significantly out of step with ordinary voters. Take abortion, for example. The *New York Times/CBS News* poll from which these data are taken identifies five possible answers to the question: 'What is your personal feeling about abortion?' As Table 5.3 shows, and contrary to what you would imagine from media coverage, which tends to focus on two extreme positions, the majority of ordinary voters are very much in the middle ground on this question.

Most voters are comfortable with abortion being available in cases of rape or incest, or if the life of the mother is in danger. Only 26% think that abortion should be available in 'all cases'. Among Democratic voters, this figure increases only marginally — to 33%. Only one-third of Democratic voters

think that abortion should be an unlimited right. But among 2008 Democratic National Convention delegates, 58% said that their personal feeling about abortion was that it should be available in all cases. Phrased another way, the poll asked respondents whether abortion should be 'generally available', 'available under stricter limits' or 'not permitted' and, as Table 5.4 shows, once again Democratic Convention delegates were significantly out of step with voters. Whereas only 43% of Democrat voters favour abortion to be 'generally available', this position was held by 70% of Democratic delegates.

Table 5.3 Answers to question: 'What is your personal feeling about abortion?'

Group	All cases (%)	With restrictions (%)	Rape, incest, save life (%)	Only to save life (%)	Not permitted (%)
All voters	26	17	32	18	4
Democrat voters	33	20	32	11	2
2008 Democrat delegates	58	18	10	2	0

Table 5.4 Answers to question: 'Which comes closest to your view on abortion?'

Group	Generally available (%)	Available under stricter limits (%)	Not permitted (%)
All voters	33	40	24
Democrat voters	43	39	16
2008 Democrat delegates	70	20	3

Nelson Polsby and Aaron Wildavsky (*Presidential Elections: Strategies and Structures of American Politics,* 2004) draw attention to this phenomenon, stating that 'the delegates may move to the ideological extremes, while the bulk of the voters out in the country remain firmly in or near the centre'. Delegates are an elite group — more educated, more professional, and wealthier than ordinary voters. They tend to be overwhelmingly either elected officials or party activists and, as Polsby and Wildavsky also point out: 'evidence from representative governments throughout the world demonstrates that voters have more moderate views than elected officials, who in turn are more moderate than party activists.'

McCain's choice of running-mate

The vice-president has two duties. One is to inquire daily as to the health of the president, and the other is to attend the funerals of Third World dictators.

Those were the rather revealing views of Senator John McCain on the office of the vice-president back in 2000 during his unsuccessful bid for the Republican presidential nomination.

In 2008, John McCain's shortlist of potential vice-presidential running-mates was quite well trailed in the media in the weeks running up to the Republican Convention. The front-runners seemed to be McCain's former rival from the primaries Mitt Romney, the Independent–Democrat senator from Connecticut Joe Lieberman, and the former Homeland Security secretary of Pennsylvania, Governor Tom Ridge. However, McCain had little personal chemistry with Romney, feared that Ridge's liberal views on abortion would further alienate the Republican base, and thought Lieberman — as a Democrat — too high a risk. He chose none of these, picking instead the Governor of Alaska, Sarah Palin. At 44, she was younger than Barack Obama and had been in office for just over 20 months, making Obama's 4 years in the US Senate seem somewhat lengthy. Before becoming Governor, Sarah Palin had been mayor of Wasilla — population (2000 census) 5,469 — the size of a typical English village. Political pundit Charlie Cook commented in his weekly Cook Report: 'Most everyone agrees that John McCain's selection of Alaskan Governor Sarah Palin as running-mate could be a 'game-changer', but they disagree over which way it might change the game.' The Lexington column in *The Economist* (6 September) described Sarah Palin as 'the woman from nowhere'.

This was the first time that the Republicans had nominated a woman to the office of the vice-presidency and the announcement's reception was reminiscent of that which greeted the announcement that Democrat Walter Mondale had chosen Geraldine Ferraro to be his running-mate back in 1984. As I wrote in the *Annual Survey 1985*:

> Ferraro's nomination was greeted with extraordinary enthusiasm in many quarters, to such an extent that for some time Mondale was in danger of being up-staged.

The initial response among rank-and-file conservative Republicans to the choice of Sarah Palin was most enthusiastic. By picking Palin, McCain had managed to do something he had thus far failed to do in his campaign, namely to solidify the conservative base of the Republican Party behind him. Palin, with her strong opposition to abortion, her support for gun rights and her born-again, evangelical faith was the immediate poster girl for conservative Republicans who thus far in 2008 had cheered wholeheartedly only for Mike Huckabee's brief brush with success in the early primaries.

However, there were three immediate drawbacks of the Palin pick. First, McCain had so far focused his campaign message on his experience versus Obama's inexperience. Now McCain was asking the country to put someone with 20 months' governmental experience, from a state with a population (around 630,000) just half that of Dallas, to be a 72-year-old heartbeat away from the Oval Office. Table 5.5 shows that a minority of voters saw Palin as qualified to become president if anything should happen to McCain.

Table 5.5 *Do you consider the vice-presidential candidate qualified to step in as president if necessary?*

Vice-presidential candidate	Year	Party	Percentage who considered them qualified for the presidency
Joe Biden	2008	Democrat	71
Lloyd Bentsen	1988	Democrat	67
Al Gore	1992	Democrat	64
Dick Cheney	2000	Republican	60
Joe Lieberman	2000	Democrat	60
John Edwards	2004	Democrat	51
Sarah Palin	**2008**	**Republican**	**45**
Dan Quayle	1988	Republican	43

Source: *Newsweek*, 22 September, 2008

Second, Palin was ideologically so far to the right that she was certainly not going to help McCain attract crucial independent voters in the swing states — Colorado, New Mexico, Ohio and the like. Some media commentators suggested initially that by choosing a woman, McCain might attract disenchanted Hillary Clinton-supporting Democrats to vote Republican. The trouble with this line of argument was that about the only thing that Mrs Clinton and Mrs Palin have in common is Mrs. Third, because McCain had decided on Palin so late in the day, the announcement was made before the McCain team had fully checked her out. Indeed, it was soon widely reported that McCain and Palin had met only once before the announcement — for just 15 minutes at a Republican governors' conference in Washington DC earlier in the year.

The Republican Convention

The Republicans were due to start their convention in Minneapolis St Paul on Monday 1 September. This was the first time that the Republicans had met in the twin cities in over a century, the last time being 1892. The first day of the proceedings was virtually wiped out by the arrival of Hurricane Gustav on the coast of Louisiana. McCain decided that television pictures of Republicans partying in Minneapolis while Louisiana was being battered by a hurricane might remind voters of the disaster of Hurricane Katrina in 2005, when the federal government fiddled while New Orleans sank. President Bush, who was due to appear at the convention on that first day, cancelled his visit and appeared briefly by video link on the Tuesday. A casual observer of the convention might not have even realised that President Bush was a member of the Republican Party. He was almost totally ignored and unmentioned. Indeed, speakers at the Democratic Convention mentioned the President more often (46 times per 25,000 words) than speakers at the Republican Convention (just 7 times per 25,000 words) (see Table 5.6). It showed the extent to which Bush was regarded as a drag on the Republican ticket in 2008.

Table 5.6 Number of times speakers used word/phrase per 25,000 words spoken at Democratic and Republican Conventions

Democratic Convention		Republican Convention	
Change	89	God	43
Opponent's name	78	Tax(es)	42
Energy	49	Business(es)	30
Bush	46	Change	30
Jobs	39	Energy	26
Healthcare	34	Opponent's name	25
Economy	32	Reforms	22
Tax(es)	26	War	20
Iraq	25	Jobs	18
God	22	Character	17
Four more years	14	Iraq	16
Business(es)	13	Economy	15
Terrorism/ist	8	Vice-President	14
Cheney	6	Terrorism/ist	8
Reform(s)	6	Bush	7

Source: www.nytimes.com

Also on Tuesday, the convention was addressed by Independent–Democrat Senator Joe Lieberman, who had been Al Gore's running-mate in the 2000 election. Lieberman had broken with the Democrats because of his support for President George W. Bush's military operations in Iraq.

Wednesday's schedule was dominated by the acceptance speech delivered by Sarah Palin. Her speech was received rapturously by the delegates as she described herself as 'an average hockey mom' who was 'going to Washington to serve the people of this great country', not to gain the approval of political reporters or commentators. Palin's speech was watched by a staggering 37 million television viewers, only 1 million fewer than watched Obama's acceptance speech the previous week. The same day saw the formality of endorsing John McCain as the party's presidential candidate. With 2,380 delegates in the hall, McCain required 1,191 votes to win an absolute majority and confirm the nomination. In the event, he was nominated almost unanimously with 2,343 (98%) of the delegates voting for McCain, 15 for Congressman Ron Paul, two for former Governor Mitt Romney and 20 delegates not voting.

Most of John McCain's former rivals from the primaries — Rudy Giuliani, Mitt Romney, Mike Huckabee, Fred Thompson and Sam Brownback — were on hand during the week to pledge their wholehearted support to McCain. The only hold-out was Congressman Ron Paul, who was offered a prime-time speaking slot in exchange for his backing of the McCain–Palin ticket but

declined to do so, choosing instead to hold a rival convention across town and continue his denunciation of the President's war in Iraq.

In his acceptance speech on the final night of the convention, John McCain tried to sell himself as the candidate of change — mentioning the word thirty times during his speech. 'Let me offer an advance warning to the old, big-spending, do-nothing, me-first, country-second Washington crowd,' rallied McCain. 'Change is coming.' The audience roared their approval as he told them: 'I don't work for a party. I don't work for a special interest. I don't work for myself. I work for you.' Obama's campaign team was quick to point out that McCain, a Senator since 1987, has been part of the 'do-nothing Washington crowd' for over 20 years. Obama's team also asked how McCain could put himself about as the candidate of change when he had supported President Bush 90% of the time in votes in the US Senate.

The Republican delegates

Just as in the Democratic Party, the positions of Republican delegates were not always in line with those of typical Republican voters, as is shown in Table 5.7. Republican delegates were more supportive of the war in Iraq and they were more conservative on abortion and gun laws, though not on gay marriage. They were also more philosophically conservative, more educated, much wealthier and far more male than typical Republican voters.

Table 5.7 Selected policy positions and personal characteristics of Republican National Convention delegates, 2008

Characteristic	All voters (%)	Republican voters (%)	Republican delegates (%)
US did the right thing in Iraq	37	70	80
Abortion should be permitted only to save life	18	27	31
Abortion should not be permitted	24	37	43
Gay couples should have no legal recognition	39	57	46
Gun laws should be less strict	11	17	38
Describe yourself as an evangelical Christian	27	39	33
Describe yourself as 'very liberal'	8	2	0
Describe yourself as 'very conservative'	15	30	40
White	83	93	93
Post-graduate educated	12	1	50
Earn over $75,000 per year	31	39	66
Male	46	44	68
National Party Conventions are still needed	56	48	89

Source: *New York Times*, 1 September 2008

On the issue of abortion, however, the views of Republican delegates were much closer to those of Republican voters than the views of Democratic delegates were to Democratic voters. Democratic delegates differed from Democratic voters by an average of 26 percentage points on the two questions on abortion, while Republican delegates differed from Republican voters by an average of only 5 percentage points. For example, whereas only 43% of Democratic voters thought abortion should be generally available to those who wanted it, 70% of Democratic delegates took that position. On the other hand, while 37% of Republican voters thought that abortion should not be permitted under any circumstances, 43% of Republican delegates took that position.

Post-Convention bounce

For decades now, opinion pollsters have been measuring the increase in popular support for a candidate just before and then immediately after their National Party Convention and thereby working out the increase in their support which might reasonably be attributed to the convention in general and the candidate's acceptance speech in particular. This increase in popular support is known as the 'bounce' and, following the 22 conventions — 11 for each party — held between 1964 and 2004, the median increase has been 5 percentage points, though as Table 5.8 shows, there have been considerable variations, from a 16-point bounce for Bill Clinton in 1992 to a 1-point decrease for John Kerry in 2004.

Table 5.8 Post-Convention bounces in percentage points, 1964–2008

Year	Democratic candidate	Post-Convention bounce	Republican candidate	Post-Convention bounce
1964	Lyndon Johnson	3	Barry Goldwater	5
1968	Hubert Humphrey	2	Richard Nixon	5
1972	George McGovern	0	Richard Nixon	7
1976	Jimmy Carter	9	Gerald Ford	5
1980	Jimmy Carter	10	Ronald Reagan	8
1984	Walter Mondale	9	Ronald Reagan	4
1988	Michael Dukakis	7	George H. W. Bush	6
1992	Bill Clinton	16	George H. W. Bush	5
1996	Bill Clinton	5	Bob Dole	3
2000	Al Gore	8	George W. Bush	8
2004	John Kerry	−1	George W. Bush	2
2008	Barack Obama	4	John McCain	6

Source: www.gallup.com

Neither Obama's 4-point bounce nor McCain's 6-point bounce was remarkable. Both were well below the bounce achieved by their respective party candidates in 2000. Obama's smaller than average bounce may simply be down to the fact that, having fought a 6-month primary battle against Hillary Clinton, so many voters had already made up their minds about him before the convention. McCain's 6-point bounce was largely attributed to his having enthused the Republican base with his selection of Sarah Palin as his vice-presidential running-mate.

The net effect of the two candidates' bounces was that McCain moved from trailing Obama in national polls before the convention to a leading position afterwards. Republicans were cock-a-hoop. They believed that they had made a significant breakthrough in the election and that the McCain–Palin ticket could go on from here to victory on 4 November.

Questions

1 What was unique about Barack Obama's announcement that Joe Biden was to be his running-mate?
2 What do the vast majority of Democratic vice-presidential candidates between 1944 and 2008 have in common?
3 What reasons are suggested for Obama's choice of Biden?
4 Write a short paragraph about the final night of the Democratic Convention and Barack Obama's acceptance speech.
5 In what ways were Democratic delegates unrepresentative of ordinary Democratic voters?
6 Who had John McCain been seriously considering as his vice-presidential running-mate? Why did he decide against them?
7 How was the announcement of Sarah Palin as McCain's running-mate greeted? Why did she appeal to the conservative base of the Republican Party?
8 What three immediate drawbacks does this chapter identify regarding the selection of Sarah Palin?
9 What conclusions can be drawn from the statistics shown in Table 5.5?
10 How did McCain try to portray himself in his acceptance speech?
11 How representative were Republican delegates of Republican voters?
12 Comment on the 'bounce' each candidate received from his party convention.

Chapter 6

The campaign

What you need to know

- The general election campaign traditionally runs from Labor Day (the first Monday in September) to the day before election day (the Tuesday after the first Monday in November) — a period of 9 weeks.
- The fortunes of the major party candidates are tracked through the frequent publication of opinion polls.
- The campaign features rallies at which the presidential and vice-presidential candidates appear, usually separately.
- Much of the campaign is conducted via the media — especially television.
- Candidates air (usually) 30-second commercials that can be either positive (about oneself and one's own policies) or negative (about one's opponent).
- The buying of airtime for these commercials is by far the biggest expense of a modern presidential campaign.
- The campaign features live television debates — three between the presidential candidates, and one between the vice-presidential candidates.

With such a late finish to the Democratic primaries and also unusually late dates for both National Party Conventions, the 2008 general election campaign began in earnest on the day after the Republican National Convention ended — Friday 5 September — and lasted for just 60 days up to election day on 4 November. What happened during these 60 days to shape the race and lead the election to its eventual conclusion?

Setting the scene

In 2004, the Republicans, with President George W. Bush, had beaten the Democratic challenger, John Kerry, by 286 Electoral College votes to 252. To win the presidency, a candidate must win 270 votes in the Electoral College. Therefore, in 2008, Barack Obama needed to hold on to all the states that John Kerry had won 4 years earlier, and then win states with at least 18 Electoral College votes. All John McCain had to do was to hold on to the states that Bush had won in 2004. He could afford to lose just 16 Electoral College votes. But unbeknown to Senator McCain, there were two ticking time bombs waiting for him down the campaign trail — one was totally outside of his control; the other was of his own making. The first was the economic

meltdown on Wall Street; the second was his selection of Sarah Palin as his vice-presidential running-mate.

McCain leads

During the first week or so of the campaign, things went well for John McCain. He came out of his convention with a more significant 'bounce' in the polls and his choice of Governor Sarah Palin of Alaska seemed to have brought his campaign to life. 'Post-Convention Contest is Even: White Women Shift to McCain' was the headline from the *ABC News/Washington Post* poll published on 8 September, just 4 days after the close of the Republican National Convention. 'John McCain's taken the better boost from the presidential nominating conventions, eroding Barack Obama's advantage on change, improving on enthusiasm, moving away from George W. Bush — and advancing among white women with the help of his surprise vice-presidential pick,' ran the poll commentary.

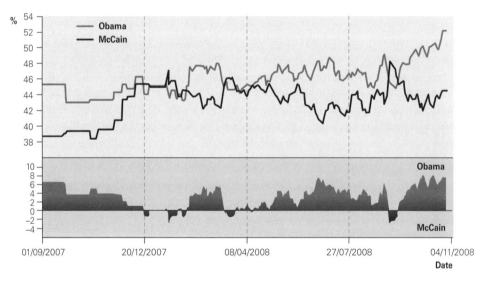

Figure 6.1 Obama vs McCain national polls: September 2007–November 2008

Source: www.realclearpolitics.com

Nationwide polls showed McCain taking the lead for the first time since mid-April (see Figure 6.1). By the beginning of the campaign's first full week, the Gallup daily tracking poll had McCain leading Obama by 5 percentage points and he held that lead for the whole week. More importantly, there were states that John Kerry had won for the Democrats in 2004 that now looked well within McCain's grasp. In 2004, Kerry had won Michigan, Minnesota, New Hampshire, Wisconsin and Pennsylvania by 3 percentage points or less. Now McCain was in a statistical dead heat with Obama in all five states. Even the New York stock market was looking rosier, with the Dow Jones Industrial Average putting on over 200 points during the week.

Wall Street collapses

This all changed on Monday 15 September — Meltdown Monday. Lehman Brothers filed for bankruptcy, the Bank of America had to come to the rescue of Merrill Lynch, and the Dow Jones plunged 499 points. That day's Gallup tracking poll had Obama and McCain in a dead heat at 47%. It was the last time that McCain reached that figure and the last day when he was not behind in that tracking poll.

McCain hadn't helped himself by saying a number of times during the campaign — and even repeating on that Monday — that 'the fundamentals of the American economy are essentially sound'. The comment might qualify for a Herbert Hoover award, reminiscent as it was of President Hoover's 1932 remark that prosperity was 'just around the corner'.

The *New York Times* editorial of the following day was not kind to McCain:

> John McCain spent Monday claiming as he had done countless times before
> — that the economy was fundamentally sound. Had he missed the collapse
> of Lehman Brothers, or the sale of Merrill Lynch? Was he unaware of the
> impending layoffs of tens of thousands of Wall Street employees on top of the
> growing numbers of unemployed workers throughout the United States?

An added problem for McCain was that his campaign was always going to do better if the focus was on national security and the 'war on terror'. Polls still showed McCain with a 20 percentage-point lead over Obama when voters were asked who they most trusted to handle terrorism. But when it came to handling the economy, McCain trailed Obama by 9 percentage points.

As Ronald Brownstein pointed out in the *National Journal* (27 September 2008), the two candidates' initial responses to the financial crisis captured their contrasting strategies in this campaign. Obama immediately released an unusual 2-minute long television commercial in which he talked directly to the camera about his economic agenda, promising 'real change', and asked viewers to read the whole plan on his website. McCain's response was a television ad that promised 'experience and leadership in a time of crisis'. Obama stressed the plan; McCain stressed the man. The entire campaign can be summed up as 'the plan vs the man' or 'change vs experience'.

The following week, as the economic crisis deepened, President Bush submitted a $700 billion bail out package to Congress that had bipartisan support. The package was put forward by Bush's treasury secretary, Hank Paulson, and was supported by the Democratic and Republican leadership in Congress. But passage through Congress was not assured. If his choice of Sarah Palin as his vice-presidential running-mate was McCain's first serious strategic mistake in this campaign, now came his second — his decision to arbitrarily suspend his campaign and return to Washington to join in the economic crisis talks at the White House. McCain suggested that unless the

bail out package was passed, he would not take part in the first of the three presidential debates scheduled for the end of that week. In the end there was no agreement on the bail out package, but McCain still showed up at the debate.

The candidates debate

As in every election for more than 20 years, the presidential candidates of the two major parties agreed to meet in three live, televised debates. The first, in Oxford, Mississippi on 26 September, was in the traditional format with the two candidates standing at lecterns facing the moderator, who on this occasion was Jim Lehrer of the PBS *NewsHour* programme. The designated topic should have played to John McCain's strengths — foreign and national security policy. But given the recent collapse of the US stock market, Lehrer decided to devote the opening third of the 90-minute debate to questions about the economy.

Both candidates equipped themselves well and there were no obvious gaffes. Lehrer tried desperately to get the two senators engaged in a genuine debate — not easy to do in this rather stilted format. But Obama did give it a shot, often turning to Senator McCain and dropping the formal title and calling him simply 'John' — a form he used 24 times during the debate. McCain, by contrast, refused to join in such informality, directed all his answers straight back at the moderator, and would not even so much as look at Senator Obama, let alone call him by his first name. The effect was to make Obama look the more open and conversational. It was, in my mind, a strategic mistake by McCain — though not one of any great or lasting significance.

What the debates did accentuate was the generational gap between the 72-year-old McCain and the 47-year-old Obama. Not only did McCain look much older but, at times, he *sounded* older. For example, at one point in the debate McCain talked about 'Reagan's SDI' having helped to end the Cold War. Ronald Reagan was first elected president in 1980 — 28 years ago. He would mean little or nothing to anyone under 40, and the term 'SDI' — the abbreviation for the Strategic Defense Initiative — would be virtually meaningless to most of the debate audience. In a *Washington Post/ABC News* poll immediately after the debate, 38% judged Obama the winner, with 24% judging McCain to have come out on top. The remainder scored it a draw (22%) or had no opinion (16%).

As in previous election cycles, the two vice-presidential candidates met in one televised debate, held in St Louis, Missouri, on 2 October. This was the most anticipated — and, unusually, the most watched — of all this year's debates. The debate attracted an audience of 73 million viewers, compared with just over 52 million for the first Obama–McCain debate. Maybe it was Americans' love of 'train-wreck television', for there was a sneaking suspicion that many had tuned in just to see if the wheels would fall off the Palin bandwagon. The

Alaskan Governor had already endured two trials by television in extended interviews, first with ABC's Charlie Gibson and then with NBC's Katie Couric. She was also being mercilessly — but brilliantly — lampooned by comedienne Tina Fey on NBC's *Saturday Night Live*. The 90-minute debate was a strange mismatch of Senate standing committee formality from the Senator and folksy platitudes, punctured by the odd wink, from the Governor. There was also an equally obvious mismatch between the questions asked by moderator Gwen Ifill and the answers given by Governor Palin. When asked about the mortgage crisis, Governor Palin proposed: 'Let's commit ourselves just everyday American people [sic], Joe Six-Pack, hockey moms across the nation.' When asked about the federal bail out plan, she replied: 'I want to go back to the energy plan.' Asked about Wall Street bankruptcies: 'I want to talk about, again, my record on energy.' Joe Six-Pack may have liked it, but Joe Biden was becoming more and more frustrated, at one point remarking: 'If you notice, Gwen, the Governor did not answer the question.' Palin's response? 'I may not answer the questions that either the moderator or you want to hear, but I'm going to talk straight to the American people.' There were also winks to the camera and, just for good measure, the odd 'darn right' and 'doggone it'. It will surely go down as the folksiest performance ever in a televised debate.

All that said, there was no train wreck: Governor Palin survived. Whether this was good news or not for Senator McCain is debatable, for it meant that the calls for her to be dropped from the Republican ticket were now muted for the remainder of the campaign.

When Obama and McCain met for their second debate — in Nashville, Tennessee, on 7 October — the format was that of a town hall meeting, with the two participants perched on bar stools and taking questions from an invited audience. The format was said to favour John McCain, who had made town hall meetings a trademark of his primary campaign earlier in the year. Against a background of falling poll numbers going into the debate, McCain had promised his supporters that he would 'take the gloves off' in this second encounter with Senator Obama. Indeed, McCain was the more aggressive of the two: striding to the centre of the stage more quickly than Obama when it was his turn to answer; getting up close to the questioners in the audience. But rather than sit while Obama spoke, McCain stood upright or leaned against his stool, 'fidgety and unsmiling' according to Dana Milbank in the next day's *Washington Post*.

Table 6.1 shows the combined effect of the first two presidential debates on voting intentions. There are two points of note. First, it is clear that most potential voters did not change their opinion of either candidate as a result of these two debates. Second, of those whose opinion did change, Obama came out on top, with 32% having a better opinion of him as a result of the debates as opposed to only 8% having a worse opinion. For McCain, while 12% had a better opinion of him following the debates, 26% had a worse opinion.

Table 6.1 Effect of first two presidential debates

Question: 'As a result of the two presidential debates that have been held do you have a better/worse opinion of Obama/McCain?'

Candidate	Better (%)	Worse (%)	Has not changed (%)	No opinion (%)
Obama	32	8	59	2
McCain	12	26	60	2

Source: ABC News/*Washington Post* poll, conducted 8–11 October

The final debate between the presidential candidates took place on 15 October at Hofstra University in Hempstead, New York, and took the format of a round-table discussion. McCain was again feisty, and came up with one of his best lines when repeatedly accused by Senator Obama of supporting President Bush's policies: 'Senator Obama, I am not President Bush. If you wanted to run against President Bush, you should have run four years ago.' But the debate was probably best remembered for the frequent references to Joe Wurzelbacher, a plumber, who had heckled Senator Obama during a recent visit to Ohio. 'Joe the Plumber' received no fewer than 23 mentions during the debate. He would even make guest appearances at subsequent McCain rallies.

This whole election year had seemed to be a battle between 'change' and 'experience'. How did these two words fair in the three presidential debates, and who used them most? The slightly surprising thing is that neither candidate used either word very much in any of the debates, although Obama did manage to give 'change' 11 mentions in the second debate. But he managed only six in the first and one in the third. McCain said the word 'change' only nine times throughout the three debates, and six of those came during the first debate. Only McCain gave 'experience' a mention — eight times in all, and six of those were in the first debate. Final Score: change 27; experience 8.

Policies

Party platforms in American presidential elections are often written off as merely a collection of generalities and statements that suggest the party is in favour of motherhood and apple pie. True, the 2008 Republican and Democratic Party platforms did contain some paragraphs that it would be quite difficult to label as distinctly Republican or Democrat. For example, one of the platforms claimed:

> Our party embodies a uniquely American spirit. It is the spirit of independent minds, the conviction that open and honest debate is essential to the freedom we enjoy as Americans.

While the other party's platform claimed:

> America must challenge us again — to serve our country and to meet our responsibilities, whether in our families, our civic organisations or our places of worship. This is the essence of what it means to be a patriot: not only to declare our love for this nation, but to show it — by deeds, our priorities, and the commitments we keep.

In case you can't work it out, the first is an extract from the Republican platform; the second from the Democratic platform.

However, in a number of policy areas the two party platforms offered some very distinct differences. Take, for example, the right to life. One party stated that:

> We strongly and unequivocally support *Roe* v *Wade* and a woman's right to choose a safe and legal abortion, regardless of ability to pay, and we oppose any and all efforts to weaken or undermine that right.

While the other stated:

> We assert the inherent dignity and sanctity of all human life and affirm that the unborn child has a fundamental individual right to life which cannot be infringed.

No bland generalities there and no need, I trust, for me to identify which is which.

When it came to civil rights, the differences may have been subtler, but they were still there:

> Democrats will fight to end discrimination based on race, sex, ethnicity, national origin, language, religion, sexual orientation, gender identity, age and disability in every corner of our country.

Democrats could easily come up with a list of ten things that should not be discriminated against. Republicans could manage only seven and had to mention the giveaway phrase 'equal opportunity':

> Our commitment to equal opportunity extends from landmark school-choice legislation to historic appointments at the highest level of government. We consider discrimination based on sex, race, age, religion, creed, disability or national origin to be immoral.

Notice the omission in the Republican list of discrimination regarding sexual orientation and gender identity.

The two campaigns were also discernibly different when it came to energy policy and especially on the policy towards further drilling for oil on American soil. The Democrats stated that 'we can't drill our way to energy independence'. Republicans, on the other hand, stated that 'if we are to have the resources we need to achieve energy independence, we simply must draw more American oil from American soil'. Or as Sarah Palin liked to put it: 'Drill, baby, drill!' In education, the Democrats stated that 'graduation from a quality public (i.e. state-run) school and the opportunity to succeed in college must be the birthright of every child — not the privilege of the few'. The Republicans 'reject the one-size-fits-all approach' to education, and 'support parental options, including home-schooling'. Differences were also seen in healthcare policy. Whereas Democrats 'are united around a commitment that every American be guaranteed affordable, comprehensive healthcare', Republicans 'believe the key to real reform is to give control of the healthcare system to patients and their healthcare providers, not bureaucrats in government or business'. Again, as in education, for Democrats it's a national plan; for Republicans it's choice.

Another topical issue in 2008 was gun ownership, following the Supreme Court's controversial decision earlier in the year. Both parties claimed to support the 2nd Amendment's right to 'bear arms'. But there were significant differences as to what restrictions they supported concerning this right. The Democratic platform stated:

> We believe that the right to own firearms is subject to reasonable regulation, but we know that what works in Chicago may not work in Cheyenne.

The Republican platform came out in full support of the Supreme Court's decision, which affirmed the right of every individual to 'bear arms' and called on the next president 'to appoint judges who will similarly respect the Constitution'.

Although John McCain's candidacy in no way represented the conservative wing of the Republican Party, there were significant policy differences between him and Barack Obama. American voters were being presented with a clear choice between the agendas of the two major parties, just as they had been in the elections of 2000 and 2004.

Money, ads and registration

During this campaign, it became very clear that Barack Obama had significant advantages over John McCain in three vital areas — money, television ads and voter registration. But in the end, it all came down to money. McCain had decided to stick with the federal dollar hand-out — $84 million from the federal government — to finance his general election campaign from September through to election day. But in accepting that cash hand-out, McCain had to agree not to spend anything beyond that. Having said initially that he would do the same, Obama changed his mind and went without the federal hand-out, meaning he could raise and spend as much as he liked. Having raised $66 million in August, Obama went on to raise a record $150 million in September, giving him a huge financial edge over McCain.

The effects were extraordinary. By the first week in October, Obama had already spent over $5 million on television ads in North Carolina. McCain had spent just over $790,000 and his 11 percentage-point lead in the state had disappeared. In Missouri, Obama had 41 offices; McCain had just 16. McCain's earlier 7 percentage-point lead in the state had evaporated. Between 28 September and 4 October, Obama outspent McCain on television ads by more than three to one in Florida and Virginia. During those 7 days, both states moved from leaning-McCain states to leaning-Obama states. As Table 6.2 shows, these were not the only states where McCain was being outspent at this crucial stage in the campaign.

Table 6.2 Television advertising spending by Obama and McCain: 28 September–4 October

State	Obama television ad spending (dollars)	McCain television ad spending (dollars)
Colorado	980,000	801,000
Florida	2,213,000	659,000
Indiana	614,000	179,000
Michigan	1,590,000	1,250,000
Missouri	492,000	193,000
New Hampshire	354,000	160,000
New Mexico	185,000	144,000
North Carolina	1,236,000	148,000
Ohio	2,218,000	1,727,000
Pennsylvania	2,202,000	1,645,000
Virginia	2,057,000	547,000
Wisconsin	1,189,000	896,000

Throughout this campaign, Obama was significantly out-raising and out-spending McCain. He was therefore able to spend money on television ads in states won by Bush in 2004 that were now competitive. Take Indiana, for example. Bush won the state in 2004 by 21 percentage points. Because it was such a solidly Republican state, neither Bush nor Kerry spent a penny on television commercials in the state 4 years ago. But by early October 2008, McCain's lead in Indiana had shrunk to around 2 percentage points and Obama was outspending him three to one on television commercials in the state.

A third area in which Obama's Democrats were enjoying a significant advantage was in voter registration. Not only had the Democrats registered significantly more voters than the Republicans during the primaries — one of the advantages of the long-running battle between Barack Obama and Hillary Clinton — but they continued this advantage into the general election as well. Take 11 key states — won by George W. Bush in 2004, but targeted by

Barack Obama in 2008: Ohio, Florida, Georgia, North Carolina, Virginia, Indiana, Missouri, Colorado, Iowa, Nevada and New Mexico; and add Pennsylvania — a state won by John Kerry in 2004, but targeted by John McCain as a possible Republican gain in 2008. Throughout these 12 key states, electoral rolls increased by about 4 million voters, a very significant amount. But there were overwhelmingly more newly registered Democrats than newly registered Republicans. In Florida, a key swing state, Democratic registration gains during 2008 were more than double those made by the Republicans. In Colorado and Nevada, the ratio was four to one, and in North Carolina it was six to one.

In some of these swing states, voter registration could have been the crucial factor that swung them from being Republican in 2004 to Democratic in 2008. Take Nevada, for example. Bush won Nevada for the Republicans in 2004 by just 21,000 votes. But in 2008, the Democrats added nearly 100,000 to the electoral roll against just 22,000 new Republicans. In New Mexico, which Bush won by just 6,000 votes in 2004, Democrats added 40,000 new voters in 2008 compared with just 12,000 new Republicans. Obama would go on to win both states.

Campaigning

For these $8\frac{1}{2}$ weeks, Barack Obama and John McCain criss-crossed the country from rally to rally. As would be expected, both parties concentrated only on the 'swing states' — states that were not clearly Democratic or Republican. Hence, if you lived in a solidly Democratic state such as California, Massachusetts or New York, you would have seen nothing at all of the campaign. The same went for those living in such solidly Republican states as Alabama, Kansas or Texas.

But what constituted a swing state changed significantly during the campaign. In early and mid-September, the swing states were principally the states won by narrow margins in 2004 — red states like Iowa, Colorado, New Mexico, Ohio or Nevada that might turn blue, and blue states like Pennsylvania, New Hampshire, Michigan, Wisconsin or Minnesota that might turn red. But by early October, most of these blue states were comfortably in Obama's column, and states previously considered safe for McCain had turned into swing states — Florida, Virginia, North Carolina, Missouri and even Indiana.

The campaigning was being done not only by Barack Obama and John McCain and their respective running-mates, but also their spouses and other party notables. Bill and Hillary Clinton both campaigned for Obama; Rudy Giuliani and Arnold Schwarzenegger both campaigned for McCain. But much of the hard work was done by volunteers, working out of the field offices in small towns all across America. A former student of mine, who had just graduated in politics at Bristol University, e-mailed me in mid-October from the Obama campaign in Virginia:

It's been a pretty terrifying, exhilarating, bizarre experience. I began by working in the campaign headquarters in Richmond. As the capital of the Old Confederacy, it was rather an interesting place to start off. After a day's instruction learning how to speak to undecided voters through canvassing and phone calls, I moved to Petersburg to join up with my field office. Petersburg is an incredibly poor, depressed place, with a very high African-American population. Though the inner city votes almost solidly Democratic, the surrounding counties are a different story. This is McCain country, and I've learnt the hard way that houses with large confederate flags, 'no trespassing' and 'beware of the dog' signs, do not take kindly to having a young English volunteer try to convince them to vote for a Harvard-educated, black Democrat.

In the final 10 days of the campaign, Obama and McCain focused on a number of critical swing states — mostly states won by George W. Bush in both 2000 and 2004, but which were now the battleground for 2008. Obama travelled over 12,000 miles during these final days to visit Nevada, Colorado, Pennsylvania, Ohio, Virginia, North Carolina, Iowa and Florida — with some states getting more than one visit. On the final day of campaigning, Obama began in Jacksonville, Florida, then went on to Charlotte, North Carolina, before ending with his final rally in Manassas, Virginia. He would win all three states the following day. John McCain's final day was even more hectic, taking in two stops in Pennsylvania before heading for Indianapolis. From there, it was off to Roswell, New Mexico, then Henderson, Nevada, and finally Prescott, Arizona — 3,685 miles in one frantic last attempt to win the election.

In terms of hostility between the candidates, this was the ninth presidential campaign I have watched and I thought it one of the most civil. McCain steadfastly refused to play the race card. The Obama campaign made no references to McCain's ethical lapses in the Keating scandal of the late 1980s. Both candidates finished the campaign with positive ratings of likeability, and both remained gracious, whether in victory or defeat, right up to the finishing line.

Why Obama won

Election night

Table 7.1 2008 presidential election results by state, showing change in the Democratic vote from 2004

State	Obama vote (%)	McCain vote (%)	Change in Democratic vote from 2004 (%)	Electoral College votes	
				Obama	McCain
Alabama	39	60	+2		9
Alaska	39	60	+3		3
Arizona	45	54	+1		10
Arkansas	39	59	−6		6
California	61	37	+7	55	
Colorado	53	45	+6	9	
Connecticut	60	39	+6	7	
Delaware	61	38	+8	3	
Florida	51	48	+4	27	
Georgia	47	52	+6		15
Hawaii	72	27	+18	4	
Idaho	36	62	+6		4
Illinois	62	37	+7	21	
Indiana	50	49	+11	11	
Iowa	54	45	+5	7	
Kansas	41	57	+5		6
Kentucky	41	57	+1		8
Louisiana	40	59	−2		9
Maine	58	40	+5	4	
Maryland	61	38	+5	10	
Massachusetts	62	36	0	12	
Michigan	57	41	+6	17	
Minnesota	54	44	+3	10	
Mississippi	43	56	+3		6
Missouri	49	50	+3		11
Montana	47	50	+8		3

State	Obama vote (%)	McCain vote (%)	Change in Democratic vote from 2004 (%)	Electoral College votes Obama	Electoral College votes McCain
Nebraska	41	57	+8	1	4
Nevada	**55**	**43**	**+7**	5	
New Hampshire	54	45	+4	4	
New Jersey	57	42	+4	15	
New Mexico	**57**	**42**	**+8**	5	
New York	62	37	+4	31	
North Carolina	**50**	**49**	**+6**	15	
North Dakota	45	53	+10		3
Ohio	**51**	**47**	**+2**	20	
Oklahoma	34	66	0		7
Oregon	57	41	+6	7	
Pennsylvania	55	44	+4	21	
Rhode Island	63	35	+3	4	
South Carolina	45	54	+4		8
South Dakota	45	53	+7		3
Tennessee	42	57	0		11
Texas	44	56	+6		34
Utah	34	63	+8		5
Vermont	67	32	+8	3	
Virginia	**52**	**47**	**+7**	13	
Washington	58	40	+5	11	
West Virginia	43	56	0		5
Wisconsin	56	42	+6	10	
Wyoming	33	65	+4		3
District of Columbia	93	7	+3	3	
Totals	**53**	**46**	**+5**	365	173

Democrat gains from 2004 in bold

For all the time and money spent on the 2008 presidential campaign, not a lot changed. By the final weeks of the campaign, the polls showed a consistent Obama lead — both in the national polls and in the projected state-by-state votes in the Electoral College. It was a question of by how much Obama would win, rather than if he would win. When the American media organisations forecast an Obama win in Pennsylvania at just after 9 p.m. Eastern Standard Time (2 a.m. GMT in the UK), it was pretty much all over. Pennsylvania had been the one large-population state that McCain had hoped to flip from the Democratic column in 2004 to the Republican column in 2008. But McCain

lost the state by 11 percentage points — a state that Kerry had won by only 2 percentage points back in 2004. Another early indication of John McCain's difficulties was that Indiana was said to be 'too close to call' —a state that George W. Bush had won by 21 percentage points 4 years earlier. The state would eventually be won by Barack Obama — one of nine red states from 2004 that turned blue in 2008 (see Table 7.1).

By the time all the results were in, we were looking at quite a different political map of the United States than the one we had seen for the last two election cycles. The maps of the 2000 and 2004 elections were almost indistinguishable, with only three states switching party control — New Hampshire, New Mexico and Iowa. This time there were nine: three down the eastern seaboard — Virginia, North Carolina and Florida; three more in the Midwest — Indiana, Ohio and Iowa; and three western states — Colorado, New Mexico and Nevada. By winning the presidential vote in the second congressional district of Nebraska, Obama added one more vote to his Electoral College tally (Nebraska is one of only two states to award its Electoral College votes by congressional district rather than on a winner-take-all basis). These nine states, plus the Nebraska district, commanded a total of 113 Electoral College votes, boosting the Democrat ticket from a losing 252 in 2004 to a winning 365 in 2008. Obama won all the states that John Kerry had won back in 2004.

But this was not a landslide election — nothing on the scale of George H. W. Bush's 426 Electoral College votes in 1988, or Reagan's 489 in 1980, and certainly not Reagan's 525 in 1984 when the Democratic ticket of Walter Mondale and Geraldine Ferraro was reduced to winning just one state, plus the District of Columbia, for 13 Electoral College votes. For all the baggage that John McCain had to carry in this election, he secured no less than 22 states with 173 Electoral College votes. McCain managed to hold on to Missouri, the first time the state has not voted for the winner since 1956. That other bellwether state, Ohio, kept up its reputation for picking winners. It has now voted for the winning candidate in all of the last 12 elections.

It was as the polls closed at 11 p.m. EST (4 a.m. GMT) in the west coast states of Washington, Oregon and California — delivering 73 Electoral College votes to Obama — that he was declared the winner of the election, a triumphant end to a 21-month quest for the presidency, resulting in the historic first of an African-American elected to the White House.

Why Obama won

So how does a 47-year-old African-American who has been in national politics for less than 4 years win the presidency of the United States? It is possible to identify six important factors that led to Obama's victory.

The two-term itch

In the election of 2008, Barack Obama had history on his side. Only twice since the civil war have Americans elected a president from the same party as the president who has just completed two full terms. The first occasion was in 1876, when Americans elected Republican Rutherford Hayes to follow two-term Republican Ulysses Grant. The second occasion was in 1988 when they elected Republican George H. W. Bush to follow two-term Republican Ronald Reagan. So for Republican John McCain to be elected after 8 years of Republican George W. Bush would have been to fly in the face of history. Also, when the Republicans won back-to-back presidencies in 1988, the outgoing incumbent, Ronald Reagan, was still popular with a majority of Americans. The same could not be said about George W. Bush in 2008.

Reasons why Obama won

- The two-term itch
- The presidency of George W. Bush
- The 'right track — wrong track' perception
- The economy
- The Palin effect
- The effectiveness of the Obama campaign

The presidency of George W. Bush

George W. Bush had been elected to office in 2000 with a promise to 'be a uniter, not a divider'. This was a phrase that Bush used often, and to good effect, during the 2000 campaign. He was trying to make a comparison with Bill Clinton, who was just completing his second term. Clinton had been an intensely divisive figure, no more so than over his impeachment by the House of Representatives in 1998 and his subsequent trial by the Senate the following year on charges of perjury and obstruction of justice. In claiming to be 'a uniter, not a divider', Bush was essentially saying: 'I'm not Bill Clinton.'

But for most of his presidency, George W. Bush has been just as divisive as his predecessor. Indeed, even the very nature of his first election divided the nation. He lost the popular vote to Democrat Al Gore by just over half-a-million votes, and was elected by the Electoral College only as a consequence of a decision made by the United States Supreme Court, of which seven of the nine justices had been appointed by Republican presidents, including two appointed by his father. 'Hail to the Thief,' protested some Democratic partisans at Bush's first inauguration in January 2001.

Bush did unite the nation following the events of 9/11, and for over 15 months he enjoyed bipartisan support, both in Congress and in the country, as Figure 7.1 shows. His approval ratings remained above 60% throughout 2002 and received two boosts in 2003 — one following the toppling of the regime of Saddam Hussein in Iraq, and another when American forces captured Saddam towards the end of the year. But during his second term, Bush became an unpopular and polarising figure as his approval ratings became toxic.

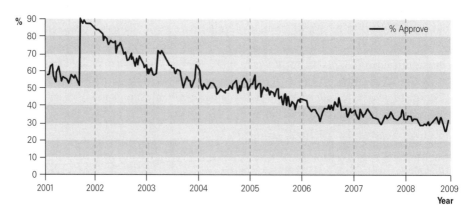

Figure 7.1 George W. Bush's approval ratings trend

Source: www.gallup.com

In 2000, Al Gore almost managed to continue the Democrats' White House tenure. But as Table 7.2 shows, the outgoing president — Bill Clinton — had high approval ratings. In the 2000 election, 57% of voters approved of Bill Clinton's performance as president. In 2008, a mere 27% of voters approved of George W. Bush's performance as president. On the back of this unpopularity, it was hardly surprising that McCain suffered defeat in 2008. Among the 27% of voters who approved of President Bush, McCain won 89–10. But among the 71% who disapproved, Obama won 67–31 — a 36 percentage-point advantage.

Table 7.2 'Do you approve or disapprove of the way the way Clinton/Bush is handling his job as president?'

Date/President	Approve (%)	Disapprove (%)
November 2000 (Clinton)	57	41
November 2004 (Bush)	53	46
November 2008 (Bush)	27	71

McCain faced an added disadvantage regarding President Bush, for although McCain was the most non-Bush candidate that the Republican Party could have nominated, the Democrats found it easy to link him with the President in the minds of voters. In 2007, *Congressional Quarterly*'s annual statistics of presidential support in Congress showed Senator McCain with a 95% presidential support score — the highest of any of the 100 senators that year. In the first presidential debate, when the discussion turned to the budget deficit, Senator Obama wasted no time in pointing out to Senator McCain: 'John, it's been your president, who you said you agreed with 90% of the time, who presided over this increase in spending.' Joe Biden rammed the point home even further in his vice-presidential debate with Sarah Palin on the issue of foreign policy:

Look, the issue is, how different is John McCain's policy going to be than George W. Bush's. I haven't heard anything yet. I haven't heard how his policy is going to be different on Iran from George W. Bush's. I haven't heard how his policy is going to be different with Israel than George W. Bush's. I haven't heard how his policy in Afghanistan is going to be different than George W. Bush's. I haven't heard how his policy in Pakistan is going to be different than George W. Bush's.

Throughout the three presidential debates between Obama and McCain, President Bush was mentioned 27 times, but it is highly significant that Obama mentioned him 21 times, McCain only six. Bush was the first incumbent president in 40 years not to make a physical appearance at his party's national convention. McCain was trying to keep the President at arm's length, and with good reason.

Table 7.3 'If John McCain were elected, would he mainly...'

Category	Total (%)	Obama (%)	McCain (%)
Continue George W. Bush's policies	48	90	8
Take the country in a different direction	48	13	85

As Table 7.3 shows, when pollsters asked election day voters: 'If John McCain were elected, would he mainly continue George W. Bush's policies, or take the country in a different direction?' voters were split 48–48, but the 48% who said he would 'mainly continue Bush's policies' split 90–8 for Obama.

The 'right track — wrong track' perception

A question pollsters often ask in the United States is: 'Do you feel things in this country are generally going in the right direction or do you feel things have pretty seriously gotten off on the wrong track?' It's referred to in shorthand as the 'right track — wrong track' question. When the *NBC News/Wall Street Journal* poll asked this question just before the 2000 election, there was a 16 percentage-point advantage in favour of the 'right track'. In 2004, there was a 6 percentage-point advantage in favour of the 'wrong track'. But in exit polls in 2008, a mere 21% said they believed the country was on the 'right track', against 75% who said it was on the 'wrong track' — a huge 54 percentage-point advantage for the wrong-trackers (see Table 7.4). Figure 7.2 shows that, from a historical perspective, these figures are quite extraordinary.

Table 7.4 'Do you think things in this country today are on the...'
(2000, 2004 and 2008 compared)

Year	Right track (%)	Wrong track (%)
2000	48	32
2004	41	47
2008	21	75

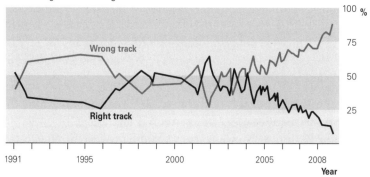

Do you feel things in this country are generally going in the right direction or are things on the wrong track?

Figure 7.2 'Right track — wrong track' poll: 1991–2008
Source: *New York Times/CBS News*

This question was highly significant in sorting out Obama and McCain supporters. The right-tracking 21% voted overwhelmingly for John McCain — 71% to 27%. But the wrong-tracking 75% voted almost equally overwhelmingly for Barack Obama — 62% to 36% (see Table 7.5). Political commentators always say that it is difficult for the incumbent White House party to win an election if the wrong trackers outnumber the right trackers. Bush managed it in 2004, but that was an exception, and the deficit was only 6 percentage points. Against a 54 percentage-point advantage for the wrong-trackers, it was difficult to see how any Republican candidate could have held the White House.

Table 7.5 'Do you think things in this country today are on the...' (2008)

Category	Total (%)	Obama (%)	McCain (%)
Right track	21	27	71
Wrong track	75	62	36

This huge majority of wrong-trackers was another reason why this election was about change, not experience. As we saw in Chapter 4, Hillary Clinton had discovered this in the Democratic primaries. She had put herself forward as the experienced candidate, but Obama had beaten her with 'change'. And in another demonstration of the impressive discipline of his campaign, Obama never let up on his theme of change. 'That's going to change when I'm president,' was an oft-repeated Obama phrase in the television debates. 'Change you can believe in' was the campaign slogan. McCain eventually tried to mimic it with his claim that 'change is coming', but the 72-year-old McCain — the man who had been in Washington for 26 years — would always struggle to sell himself as the agent of change.

Table 7.6 'Which one of these qualities mattered most in deciding how you voted for president?'

Category	Total (%)	Obama (%)	McCain (%)
Can bring about needed change	34	89	9
Shares my values	32	30	65
Has the right experience	20	7	93
Cares about people like me	12	74	24

Table 7.6 shows that 'bringing about needed change' was the number one determinant of how people voted. Of the 34% for whom that was the most important quality, 89% voted for Obama. McCain had an equally impressive lead on experience, but far fewer voters had that as their number one determinant. Neither was 2008 a 'values' election, as both 2000 and 2004 had been. Again, had it been so, McCain would have won hands down. Of those voters who said that the most important candidate quality was that he 'shares my values', McCain had a 35 percentage-point lead.

The economy

Republican vice-presidential candidate Sarah Palin liked to whip up audiences on the campaign trail in support of 'drilling for oil on American soil' with the slogan 'drill, baby, drill!' But in the words of Jennifer Granholm, the Democratic Governor of Michigan — 'Forget drill, baby, drill, here it's jobs, baby, jobs.' In exit polls, only 7% of voters said that energy policy was the most important issue for them in this election, and a massive 63% said it was the economy (see Table 7.7). Back in 2004, just 20% of voters had said the economy was the single most important issue in determining their vote.

Table 7.7 'Which of these issues is the most important facing the country?' (2008)

Category	Total (%)	Obama (%)	McCain (%)
The economy	63	53	44
The war in Iraq	10	59	39
Terrorism	9	13	86
Healthcare	9	73	26
Energy policy	7	50	46

Table 7.8 'Do you think the condition of the nation's economy is...' (2004 and 2008 compared)

Category	2004 (%)	2008 (%)
Excellent	4	1
Good	43	6
Not so good	35	44
Poor	17	49

Table 7.9 'Do you think the condition of the nation's economy is...' (2008)

Category	Total (%)	Obama (%)	McCain (%)
Excellent/good	7	26	72
Not so good/poor	93	54	44

Exit pollsters also asked voters in 2008 to describe the US economy as either excellent, good, not so good, or poor. Just 1% of voters said 'excellent', a mere 6% described it as 'good', 44% said 'not so good' and 49% said 'poor'. Table 7.8 shows how the situation had deteriorated since 2004. Table 7.9 sorts the 2008 answers into just two categories — excellent/good and not so good/poor and then shows how those two categories of voters cast their ballots. Among the mere 7% of voters who described the US economy as excellent/good, McCain had a 72–26 advantage. But among those 93% of voters who described the economy as not so good/poor, Obama held a 10 percentage-point lead, easily enough to secure his election. In a number of the states that Obama flipped from red to blue in this election, his percentage-point lead on this question was even greater — 13 points in Colorado, 14 in Iowa, 18 in Nevada and 22 points in New Mexico. Likewise, Obama had a huge advantage in this category in states that McCain had hoped to flip from blue to red, but failed — 17 points in Pennsylvania and a whopping 20 points in Michigan.

If the picture was grim for McCain in terms of the national economy, it was no better in terms of the personal economy. Exit polls asked voters, 'How worried are you that the current economic crisis will harm your family's finances over the next year?' In response, 81% of voters were worried and just 18% were not. Among the 81% of worried voters, Obama had an 18 percentage-point lead of 58–40 (see Table 7.10).

Table 7.10 'How worried are you that the current economic crisis will harm your family's finances over the next year?' (2008)

Category	Total (%)	Obama (%)	McCain (%)
Worried	81	58	40
Not worried	18	35	61

Table 7.11 'How confident are you in Obama's/McCain's ability to make the right decisions about the current economic crisis?'

Category	Obama (%)	McCain (%)
Very confident	23	14
Somewhat confident	35	34
Not too confident	21	28
Not at all confident	20	23

As we saw in Chapter 6, the American banking system collapsed right in the middle of the presidential campaign, shifting the focus of the campaign onto the economy — not McCain's strongest suit. Indeed, in an interview with the *Boston Globe* back in December 2007, McCain had admitted to reporters that 'the issue of economics is not something I've understood as well as I should'. When the *New York Times/CBS News* pre-election poll (10–13 October) asked respondents the question: 'How confident are you in John McCain's ability to make the right decisions about the current economic crisis?' 48% said they were very or somewhat confident while 51% said they were not too confident or not at all confident. When asked the same question about Barack Obama, 58% were very or somewhat confident and only 41% said they were not too confident or not at all confident (see Table 7.11).

The Palin effect

The first thing to say about the choice of Palin as vice-presidential candidate is that it hurt McCain at the polls. In its post-election edition, *The Economist* described McCain's selection of Palin as 'the worst single decision of the 2008 election season'. In answer to the question: 'Which vice-presidential candidate is qualified to become president should it become necessary?' 66% judged Joe Biden qualified but only 38% judged Sarah Palin qualified. Of the 60% who judged her 'not qualified', 81% voted for Obama and only 16% for McCain.

In the minds of many voters, the selection of Sarah Palin called into question John McCain's ability to make sound decisions. Obama held an 8 percentage-point lead in exit polls in answer to the question: 'Which candidate do you think has the right judgement to make a good president?' To many, McCain's selection of Palin looked like bad judgement on his part.

In selecting Palin, McCain was trying to be someone he wasn't and in doing so he lost some of his authenticity. Up to that point, McCain had been bashing away at Obama as too inexperienced for high office. In selecting the inexperienced governor of a small-population state as his running-mate, McCain blew a hole in his own argument.

The Palin selection was also a recipe for disunity in the Republican presidential campaign. McCain picked Palin as a fellow maverick, but the trouble with mavericks is that they don't stick to the script. Before long, Palin was throwing red meat to Republican audiences, which was clearly out of key with the McCain script. The campaign ended with open sniping between the McCain and Palin camps over anything from the extent of Palin's gaffes to the cost of her wardrobe. The McCain staff leaked to the press that Palin had 'gone rogue' and that she 'takes no advice from anyone'.

The effectiveness of the Obama campaign

From the analysis so far it almost appears as if any Democratic candidate could have won this election, for surely Hillary Clinton or John Edwards would have benefited from a two-term itch, an unpopular incumbent, a wrong-track perception in the country, a failing economy and McCain's selection of Governor Palin. To some extent, that might be correct.

But this wasn't simply a Democrat winning the White House. This was a historic win for a Democrat, and not just because of Obama's race. This was the first presidential election since 1964 in which a Democrat gained over 51% of the popular vote. For the past ten elections, no Democrat managed more than the 50.1% gained by Jimmy Carter in 1976. There were also some historic firsts in the state-by-state results. Obama was the first Democrat to win in Indiana and Virginia since 1964; the first Democrat to win an Electoral College vote in Nebraska since 1964; and the first Democrat to win North Carolina since 1976 — something that even the entirely southern ticket of Bill Clinton (Arkansas) and Al Gore (Tennessee) failed to achieve in either 1992 or 1996. Barack Obama is also the first northern liberal to win the White House since JFK in 1960.

It is true that Senator Obama had far more money available to him than did Senator McCain. By mid-October, the Federal Election Commission was reporting that through the primaries and the general election, Obama had received $639 million in campaign contributions to McCain's $335 million. Obama had therefore out-raised McCain to the tune of $304 million, compared with Bush's out-raising Kerry in 2004 by just $26 million. This gave Obama a huge advantage in the closing weeks of the campaign in terms of his ability to get his message across. During the week of 13–19 October, for example, Obama spent $39 million on television ads versus about $11.9 million for the McCain campaign. 'McCain is in a shouting match with a man with a megaphone,' commented Evan Tracey of TNS Media Intelligence, an organisation that tracks advertising spending.

This advantage showed itself in swing states. During that same week, Obama spent $2.1 million in North Carolina against McCain's $1.4 million, a state that Obama ended up winning by just 14,000 votes out of over 4.2 million cast. In Florida, Obama spent $4.6 million that week compared with McCain's $1.4 million. Obama won the state by around 200,000 votes out of over 8 million. In Indiana, Obama spent $1.8 million while McCain spent nothing at all. Obama won that state by 26,000 votes out of 2.7 million. As Ken Goldstein, director of the University of Wisconsin's advertising project, explained:

> Presidential campaigns usually have to make tough choices: If I advertise here, I can't advertise there. If I spend this money on TV, I can't spend this much money on field organisation. But Obama didn't have to make these tough choices. He could spend on TV, he could spend on radio, he could spend on field organisation, he could spend on mailing.

When it came to field organisation — that is offices and manpower in each of the states — Obama again had a significant edge. 'Obama has 40 local offices in my state of New Mexico — 40!' exclaimed Governor Bill Richardson of New Mexico — another state that Obama flipped from red to blue. McCain said he had 'about a dozen' offices in the state. In North Carolina, Obama had 47 offices against around 20 for McCain. When Indiana, a state Bush won by 21 points in 2004, suddenly became a swing state late in the campaign, McCain opened a handful of offices across the state. Obama already had 47.

The Obama campaign was also viewed as a more positive campaign than McCain's. Like Ronald Reagan in the 1980s, Obama seemed to appeal more to voters' better natures and optimism. He never appeared angry or pessimistic, despite the economic chaos going on around him. When asked in exit polls, 'Did either of the candidates attack the other unfairly?' while 49% thought that of Obama, 64% thought it of McCain.

Obama's campaign was an impressively disciplined operation. It barely put a foot wrong throughout. There was none of the infighting or backbiting seen in the Hillary Clinton campaign during the Democratic primaries, and in the McCain–Palin camp during the general election. The way Team Obama focused its resources was impressive. Take the way it won the Electoral College vote from the second district of Nebraska by focusing on the city of Omaha, upon which the district is based. Nebraska is a solidly red state: it hasn't voted Democratic in a presidential election for over 40 years; but Obama saw the possibility of one extra Electoral College vote in the state being another of the many routes to getting to the 270 votes he required. In the end, of course, he didn't need Nebraska's vote, but nothing was left to chance. If the Obama presidency shows this much attention to detail, the new White House should be a highly efficient organisation.

But the Obama campaign's effectiveness wasn't just about organisation, it was about inspiration and good judgement. 'Barack Obama has prospered in this campaign,' commented Joe Klein in *Time* magazine ('Why Barack Obama Is Winning', 22 October), 'because of the steadiness of his temperament and the judicious quality of his decision-making.' At the crucial turning point of the campaign — the onset of the economic crisis in mid-September — it was, according to Klein, 'Obama's steadiness that won the public's trust, and quite possibly the election.' While John McCain was grandstanding on the national media by suspending his campaign and threatening to pull out of the imminent television debate, Obama reacted with calmer judgement. Even when some of his advisers were telling Obama to follow McCain's lead, he refused, choosing to continue the campaign and to issue a statement suggesting that 'a president has to be able to do more than one thing at a time'. As with the vice-presidential selection, McCain looked rash and hasty; Obama looked steady and statesmanlike.

Barack Obama is no Bill Clinton. Some would read that statement as a weakness, but I am suggesting it is a strength. According to Joe Klein, unlike

Clinton, Obama 'is not childishly egomaniacal. He does not seem needy. He seems to be grown-up, in a nation that badly needs some adult supervision'. When exit polls asked voters: 'Which candidate do you think has the right judgement to make a good president?' 43% said Barack Obama while 36% said John McCain. Of the 43%who thought Obama had the better judgement, 98% voted for him. Of the 36% who thought McCain had the better judgement, again, 98% voted for him (see Table 7.12). Good judgement was clearly a strong indicator of voting intentions.

Table 7.12 'Which candidate do you think has the right judgement to make a good president?'

Category	Total (%)	Obama (%)	McCain (%)
Only Barack Obama	43	98	2
Only John McCain	36	2	98
Both of them	13	64	34
Neither of them	6	27	56

Who voted for whom in 2008?

Table 7.13 shows a breakdown of who voted for whom in this presidential race and compares the figures in each category with voting in 2004. The first thing that is clear is that Barack Obama increased the Democrats' share of the vote in almost every category, with the two exceptions being Democrats and voters aged 60 and over.

Gender

In the popular vote overall, Obama increased the Democratic share by 5 percentage points — up from 48% for Kerry in 2004 to 53% in 2008. The increase was the same among both male and female voters. Obama might have done better among women voters had 16% of those who voted for Hillary Clinton in the Democratic primaries not voted for John McCain. One suspects that a good proportion of that 16% were women. But Obama was far more popular among women voters than with men— among women, Obama beat McCain 56–43, but among men only 49–48. His 56% support from women voters was the highest for any Democrat for over 40 years. The gender gap was back.

Race

Exit poll data revealed some interesting themes in voting by race. First, this was the fifth consecutive presidential election in which the percentage of votes cast by white voters declined. In 1992, 87% of voters were white. By 2008, this figure had fallen to 74%. Obama attracted a very similar proportion of the white vote (43%) to both Kerry in 2004 (41%) and Gore in 2000 (42%).

Table 7.13 Who voted for whom?
2008 and 2004 compared

Category	2008		2004		Change in Democratic vote since 2004 (%)
	Obama (%)	McCain (%)	Kerry (%)	Bush (%)	
All (100)	53	46	48	51	+5
Men (47)	49	48	44	55	+5
Women (53)	56	43	51	48	+5
Whites (74)	43	55	41	58	+2
African-Americans (13)	95	4	88	11	+7
Hispanics/Latinos (9)	67	31	57	43	+10
White men (36)	41	57	38	61	+3
White women (39)	46	53	45	55	+1
Black men (5)	95	5	86	13	+9
Black women (7)	96	3	90	10	+6
Aged 18–29 (18)	66	32	54	45	+12
Aged 30–44 (29)	52	46	46	53	+6
Aged 45–59 (37)	50	49	48	51	+2
Aged 60+ (16)	45	53	46	54	−1
All Protestant (54)	45	54	40	59	+5
White Protestant (42)	34	65	32	67	+2
Born-again/Evangelicals (38)	41	57	34	65	+7
Catholic (27)	54	45	47	52	+7
Jewish (2)	78	21	74	25	+4
Democrats (39)	89	10	89	11	0
Republicans (32)	9	90	6	93	+3
Independents (29)	52	44	49	48	+3
Liberal (22)	89	10	85	13	+4
Moderate (44)	60	39	54	45	+6
Conservatives (34)	20	78	15	84	+5
East (21)	59	40	56	43	+3
Midwest (24)	54	44	48	51	+6
South (32)	45	54	42	58	+3
West (22)	57	40	50	49	+7
Cities over 50,000 (30)	63	35	54	45	+9
Suburbs (49)	50	48	47	52	+3
Small town/rural (21)	45	53	42	57	+3

Category	2008		2004		Change in Democratic vote since 2004 (%)
	Obama (%)	McCain (%)	Kerry (%)	Bush (%)	
Family income					
Under $15,000 (6)	73	25	63	36	+10
$15–30,000 (12)	60	37	57	42	+3
$30–50,000 (19)	55	43	50	49	+5
$50–75,000 (21)	48	49	43	56	+5
$75–100,000 (15)	51	48	45	55	+6
$100–150,000 (14)	48	51	42	57	+6
$150–200,000 (6)	48	50	42	57	+6
Over $200,000 (6)	52	46	35	64	+17
2004 voters					
Kerry (D) (37)	89	9	–	–	
Bush (R) (46)	17	82	–	–	
Others (4)	66	24	–	–	
Did not vote (13)	71	27	–	–	

Table 7.13 shows that white voters preferred John McCain by a 12 percentage-point margin, 55% to 43%. But this figure varied widely from state to state. In more liberal states such as California and Massachusetts, Obama won a majority of the white vote — by 6 percentage points in California and by 15 percentage points in Massachusetts. But in parts of the South, the white vote remained overwhelmingly Republican.

Table 7.14 Percentage change in Democratic white vote in the South: 2004–08

State	White vote 2008		White vote 2004		Percentage change in Democratic white vote
	Obama (%)	McCain (%)	Kerry (%)	Bush (%)	
Louisiana	14	84	24	75	−10
Alabama	10	88	19	80	−9
Arkansas	30	68	36	63	−6
Mississippi	11	88	14	85	−3
Georgia	23	76	23	70	0
Oklahoma	29	71	29	77	0
Florida	42	56	42	57	0
Tennessee	34	63	34	63	0
South Carolina	26	73	22	78	+4
Virginia	39	60	32	68	+7
North Carolina	35	64	27	73	+8

As shown in Table 7.14, McCain won 88% of the white vote in both Alabama and Mississippi. In four southern states — Louisiana, Alabama, Arkansas and Mississippi — the share of the Democratic vote among white voters declined from 2004. So in Louisiana, for example, whereas in 2004 John Kerry won 24% of the white vote, in 2008 Barack Obama won only 14%.

Age

As expected, Obama picked up a huge majority among young voters. Among the 18–29 age group, Obama had a 34 percentage-point lead, up 12 percentage points from the lead John Kerry had in this age group in 2004. No Democrat has captured anything like the 66% of this age group that Obama won. During the last 10 elections, John Kerry with 54% in 2004 and Bill Clinton with 53% in 1996 were the next highest. But there was no clear evidence that young people had turned out to vote in significantly larger numbers this time around. The 18–29 age group accounted for 17% of the electorate in 2004 and 18% in 2008.

Religion

Frequency of attendance at religious services has been a significant determinant of voting in recent presidential elections. One of the reasons why this was particularly marked in 2000 and 2004 was because George W. Bush is a born-again Christian and therefore attracted high levels of support from like-minded voters, who make up a significant proportion of the electorate. But if the gender gap was widening in 2008, the God gap was closing. Table 7.15 shows that among those who attend religious services weekly or more frequently — the top two categories in the table — voting in 2008 was much less polarised than in 2004. For example, in 2004 the Democrats had a 29 percentage-point deficit among those who attended religious services more than once a week. In 2008, their deficit was only 12 percentage points. It was a similar story with those who went 'weekly'. In the meantime, things were actually more polarised among the godless. Whereas in 2004 the Republicans had a 26 percentage-point deficit among those who never attended religious services, this had widened to a 37 percentage-point deficit in 2008. Obama voters were both more godly and more godless than Kerry voters in 2004.

Table 7.15 'How often do you attend religious services?' 2004 and 2008 compared

	2008			2004		
Category	Obama (%)	McCain (%)	Percentage difference	Kerry (%)	Bush (%)	Percentage difference
More than weekly	43	55	12	35	64	29
Weekly	43	55	12	41	58	17
A few times a month	53	46	7	49	50	1
A few times a year	59	40	19	54	45	9
Never	67	30	37	62	36	26

Clearly the fact that John McCain had no strong links with the religious right caused a significant decline in his support among evangelical Christians — McCain's 57% support among that group was on a par with that won by Bob Dole in 1996, the last non-evangelical Republican candidate. Back then, Dole managed 56% support among evangelicals, just 1 percentage point less than McCain's. No evidence here that Sarah Palin — a born-again, evangelical Christian — attracted large numbers of such voters to support the Republican ticket. In an election where economic rather than moral issues were uppermost in voters' minds, it was always more likely that the religious vote would be more evenly divided than in the previous two elections, when so-called moral issues had been more prominent.

Party and ideology
Both Obama and McCain attracted virtually the same level of support among their own party — with 89% of Democrats voting for Obama and 90% of Republicans voting for McCain. For Obama, this was the same level of support attracted by John Kerry from Democrats in 2004; for John McCain, it represented a 3 percentage-point fall from the 93% support George W. Bush had enjoyed, meaning that the 'Palin effect' in energising the party base was not significant.

In terms of party, the Democrats won this election for two simple reasons: far more Democrats turned out than Republicans; and independents split in Obama's favour. In 2004, both parties attracted support from 37% of the electorate. In 2008, the Democrats had pushed up to 39% while the Republicans had fallen back to 32%, opening up a 7-point advantage for the Democrats. In 2004, independent voters had divided 49–48 between Kerry and Bush; in 2008 they divided 52–44 between Obama and McCain.

Much the same was true when looking at the ideology of voters. While the make-up of the electorate hardly changed at all, Obama increased the Democratic share of support since 2004 among all three ideological groups — among liberals by 4 points, among conservatives by 5 points, and among moderates by 6 points. Whereas Kerry had a 9 percentage-point advantage among moderate voters in 2004, Obama opened up a 21 percentage-point lead among moderates in 2008.

Region
Obama increased Democratic Party support in all four regions of the country, least in the East and South, most in the Midwest. The East and West remained blue, and the South remained red, but the Midwest flipped from red to blue. A region that Bush had won by just 3 percentage points in 2004 now voted for Obama by 10 percentage points in 2008. The Democrats' 54% of the vote in the Midwest was their best in any election for over 40 years.

With victories in Virginia, North Carolina and Florida, there were also signs of a Democratic resurgence in the South, even without a southerner on the ticket. Previous Democratic tickets that had no southerner on them — Mondale/Ferraro in 1984, McGovern/Shriver in 1972 — had failed to win more than a single state, and absolutely nothing in the South.

Population area

Barack Obama made significant gains in urban areas. In cities with over 50,000 inhabitants, he increased the Democratic share of the vote by 9 percentage points over 2004, winning 63% of the vote in these population areas. Indeed, in cities over 500,000, Obama attracted 70% of the vote — up 10 percentage points on Kerry's vote there in 2004. At the same time, Obama managed to improve on Kerry's showing in suburban America. In 2004, the suburbs broke for George W. Bush 52–47, but in 2008 Obama came out on top 50–48. Obama even managed to close the deficit gap in small towns and rural America — Kerry had a 15 percentage-point deficit in 2004, but Obama shrank that to an 8-point gap in 2008.

Family income

Obama increased his party's support in every economic group and saw the largest increases at the two extremes of the scale — both those earning less than $15,000 a year and those earning over $200,000 a year. Obama thus increased Democrats' support among both the Wal-Mart and Starbucks voters. His support among the lowest economic bracket was 10 percentage points higher than John Kerry achieved in 2004. Given Obama's difficulties in attracting these voters in the Democratic primaries — they tended to over-whelmingly support Hillary Clinton — Obama did well to woo them back.

Turnout

Table 7.16 Percentage of the eligible electorate who voted in presidential elections: 1960–2008

Year	Number who voted	Percentage who voted
1960	68,838,219	67.0
1964	70,645,592	64.0
1968	73,211,875	61.0
1972	77,718,554	57.1
1976	81,555,889	55.0
1980	86,515,221	54.7
1984	92,659,600	55.9
1988	91,594,805	53.3
1992	104,428,377	58.3
1996	96,277,872	51.4
2000	105,399,313	54.2
2004	122,265,430	60.6
2008	127,500,000*	61.0*

* estimated

Source: Center for the Study of the American Electorate, press release, 6 November 2008

For all the pre-election talk about the likelihood of a record turnout, the initial research available showed that turnout levels were almost identical to those of 4 years earlier. According to statistics released by the Center for the Study of the American Electorate (CSAE), the turnout in 2008 will, when all the absentee ballots are counted, be somewhere between 60.7% and 61.7%. The final turnout figure in 2004 was 60.6% (see Table 7.16).

Table 7.17 Partisan turnout trends: 1960–2008

Year	Democratic share of the vote (%)	Republican share of the vote (%)	Third parties' share of the vote (%)
1960	32.3	32.2	0.6
1964	38.6	24.2	0.2
1968	26.5	26.9	8.6
1972	21.2	34.4	1.0
1976	27.6	26.5	1.1
1980	22.4	27.8	4.5
1984	22.7	32.9	0.4
1988	24.2	28.3	0.5
1992	25.0	21.8	11.4
1996	25.3	21.0	5.2
2000	26.3	26.0	2.0
2004	28.5	30.0	0.5
2008	31.3	28.7	0.8

Source: Center for the Study of the American Electorate, press release, 6 November 2008

Table 7.18 The ten largest increases and decreases in turnout, by state

State	Convenience voting available?	Won by	2004 turnout (%)	2008 turnout (%)	Increase (%)
10 largest increases					
North Carolina	Yes	Obama	56.8	66.3	16.6
Georgia	Yes	McCain	54.7	61.3	12.0
South Carolina	No	McCain	52.2	58.2	11.6
Alabama	No	McCain	56.3	61.6	9.4
Indiana	No	Obama	54.7	59.7	9.1
Nevada	Yes	Obama	55.3	58.8	6.3
Missouri	No	McCain	64.6	67.4	4.3
Mississippi	No	McCain	54.1	56.4	4.2
Tennessee	Yes	McCain	55.7	57.9	4.1
Virginia	No	Obama	59.9	62.2	3.9

State	Convenience voting available?	Won by	2004 turnout (%)	2008 turnout (%)	Decrease (%)
10 largest decreases					
New York	No	Obama	58.8	55.4	5.8
Hawaii	Yes	Obama	48.5	45.3	6.5
Vermont	Yes	Obama	65.5	61.1	6.7
Maryland	Yes	Obama	61.0	56.9	6.8
New Hampshire	Yes	Obama	70.0	65.2	6.9
West Virginia	Yes	McCain	53.4	49.6	7.2
Ohio	Yes	Obama	66.5	61.1	8.2
Utah	Yes	McCain	61.4	56.0	8.8
Maine	Yes	Obama	73.3	64.4	12.2
Arizona	Yes	McCain	53.0	45.8	13.5

Source: Center for the Study of the American Electorate, press release, 6 November 2008

The CSAE report suggested that the reason for the smaller than expected increase in turnout was probably due to a lower than predicted turnout among Republican voters. Curtis Gans, Director of CSAE, attributed the downturn in Republican voting to three factors. First, John McCain's efforts to unite the differing factions within the party by the nomination of Governor Sarah Palin as vice-presidential nominee 'were a singular failure'. By election day, many culturally conservative Republicans still did not see McCain as like-minded and stayed at home, while many moderate Republicans saw the Palin nomination as reckless and also stayed at home. Second, as election day approached, there was an inevitability in the national polls of a comfortable Obama win, which further discouraged Republican turnout. Third, in so far as the enthusiasm factor was concerned, this election was the mirror image of 2004. Four years ago, Republicans were very enthusiastic about President Bush but Democrats remained somewhat lukewarm towards John Kerry. But in 2008, it was the Democrats who were fired up, not the Republicans. No matter how good the Republican get-out-the-vote organisation was, it couldn't overcome the lack of enthusiasm that many Republicans felt towards John McCain. Exit polls showed that whereas 30% of voters were 'excited' about Barack Obama becoming president, only 14% felt the same way about John McCain.

As Table 7.17 shows, not only did the Republican share of the vote decrease by 1.3% from 2004, but the Democratic Party achieved its seventh successive increase in the share of the vote, from its low-point of 22.4% in 1980 to this year's 31.3%.

Of the 46 states plus the District of Columbia that were covered in the CSAE statistics, turnout was up in only 22 states and the District of Columbia.

Because of extensive use of absentee balloting in Alaska and California, all-mail voting in Oregon and most of Washington state, these states were not counted in the statistics. Table 7.18 shows the 10 states with the largest increases and decreases in turnout in this election. There are three points worth noting from these statistics. First, increases in voting came both in competitive states such as North Carolina and Indiana, but also in uncompetitive states such as Alabama and Tennessee. Second, there is little evidence that convenience voting increases turnout — by convenience voting we mean early voting, and no-excuse absentee voting whereby voters can apply for an absentee ballot without having to give a reason for not being able to vote in person. Of the ten states seeing the largest percentage increase in voting, only four had convenience voting. But of the ten states seeing the largest percentage decrease in voting, nine offered convenience voting. Third, those states with the highest increase were mostly states won by McCain, while the states with the highest decrease were mostly states won by Obama, possibly the reverse of what one might have expected.

Conclusions

'In the end, this election was driven by deep economic concerns and the prevailing emotional climate,' commented Curtis Gans of the CSAE. Clearly this was the election that was waiting to be won by the Democrats. Any Republican candidate would have found 2008 an uphill struggle. The selection by the Republicans of a more moderate, maverick, non-Bush candidate in John McCain gave them their best shot of winning. If Dick Cheney had run, as the incumbent vice-president did in 1960, 1988 and 2000 when the incumbent president was term-limited, one fears that the Republican ticket might have been reduced to winning Cheney's home state of Wyoming with its three Electoral College votes and little else.

Obama won this election by attracting a significantly greater proportion of young voters (up 12%), Hispanics (up 10%) and big-city dwellers (up 10%), as well as more independents, more very poor and very rich voters and more Midwesterners. He won the suburbs and increased the Democratic share of the vote. He won because voters, believing the country was on the wrong track, wanted to turn the country in a different direction. They were worried about both the national and personal economies and trusted Obama more than McCain to improve their economic situation. Finally, they believed that Obama possessed both the better judgement and the better team to run the country for the next 4 years.

Obama enters office with a huge amount of popular support (see Table 7.19). His 52.6% of the popular vote is not a landslide, but it is the highest share of the popular vote for any incoming president in 20 years, and the second highest since Eisenhower's 55% in 1952. Obama enters office with a much more significant mandate than Richard Nixon, Bill Clinton or George W. Bush.

But then George H. W. Bush's 53% mandate in 1988 was the beginning of what turned out to be a one-term presidency.

Table 7.19 Share of the popular vote for first-term presidents: 1960–2008

Year	President	Party	Share of vote (%)
1960	John Kennedy	Democrat	49.7
1968	Richard Nixon	Republican	43.4
1976	Jimmy Carter	Democrat	50.1
1980	Ronald Reagan	Republican	50.7
1988	George H. W. Bush	Republican	53.4
1992	Bill Clinton	Democrat	42.3
2000	George W. Bush	Republican	47.9
2008	Barack Obama	Democrat	52.6

How will Obama fare? There are, I believe, four important things he must do to give his presidency a chance of success. First, he must remember that he no longer represents the state of Illinois, where 47% of voters are Democrats. He is now president of the United States, and of all 50 states, not just those who voted for him on 4 November. Second, he must choose his White House staff and his cabinet wisely. He must avoid the bean counting and inexperience that shackled the two previous Democratic administrations of Jimmy Carter and Bill Clinton. Third, he must keep up his dialogue with the American people and try to manage the high expectations that people will inevitably have of his administration. Fourth, he needs to work in a bipartisan way with Congress, trying to achieve Republican as well as Democratic support for his major legislative initiatives. None of this will be easy, but these factors will decide whether Barack Obama becomes George H. W. Obama or Franklin Delano Obama.

Who's who in US politics 2009

Executive branch

President	Barack Obama
Vice-President	Joe Biden

The cabinet

Secretary of State	Hillary Clinton
Secretary of Defense	Robert Gates
Secretary of the Treasury	Timothy Geithner
Secretary of Agriculture	Tom Vilsack
Secretary of the Interior	Ken Salazar
Attorney General (Justice Department)	Eric Holder
Secretary of Commerce	Bill Richardson
Secretary of Labor	Hilda Solis
Secretary of Health and Human Services	Tom Daschle
Secretary of Education	Arne Duncan
Secretary of Housing and Urban Development	Shaun Donovan
Secretary of Transportation	Ray LaHood
Secretary of Energy	Steven Chu
Secretary of Veterans' Affairs	Eric Shinseki
Secretary of Homeland Security	Janet Napolitano

Executive Office of the President personnel

White House Chief of Staff	Rahm Emanuel
Director of Office of Management and Budget	Peter Orszag
Director of National Economic Council	Larry Summers
Chairman of Council of Economic Advisers	Christina Romer
Domestic Policy Council Director	Melody Barnes
National Security Adviser	James Jones
Assistant to the President for Legislative Affairs	Philip Schiliro
Trade Representative	Ron Kirk
Press Secretary	Robert Gibbs

Other executive branch personnel

Director of Central Intelligence Agency (CIA)	*
Director of Federal Bureau of Investigation (FBI)	Robert Mueller (to 2011)
Chairman of the Joint Chiefs of Staff (JCS)	Admiral Michael Mullen (to September 2009)

[* not known at time of going to print]

Legislative branch

President *Pro Tempore* of the Senate	Robert Byrd (D–West Virginia)
Senate Majority Leader	Harry Reid (D–Nevada)
Senate Minority Leader	Mitch McConnell (R–Kentucky)
Senate Majority Whip	Dick Durbin (D–Illinois)
Senate Minority Whip	Lamar Alexander (R–Tennessee)
Speaker of the House of Representatives	Nancy Pelosi (D–California)
House Majority Leader	Steny Hoyer (D–Maryland)
House Minority Leader	John Boehner (R–Ohio)
House Majority Whip	James Clyburn (D–South Carolina)
House Minority Whip	Eric Cantor (R–Virginia)

Senate Standing Committee chairs

Agriculture, Nutrition and Forestry	Tom Harkin	Iowa
Appropriations	Daniel Inouye	Hawaii
Armed Services	Carl Levin	Michigan
Banking, Housing and Urban Affairs	Christopher Dodd	Connecticut
Budget	Kent Conrad	North Dakota
Commerce, Science and Transportation	John Rockefeller	West Virginia
Energy and Natural Resources	Jeff Bingaman	New Mexico
Environment and Public Works	Barbara Boxer	California
Finance	Max Baucus	Montana
Foreign Relations	John Kerry	Massachusetts
Health, Education, Labor and Pensions	Edward Kennedy	Massachusetts
Homeland Security and Governmental Affairs	Joseph Lieberman	Connecticut
Judiciary	Patrick Leahy	Vermont
Rules and Administration	Dianne Feinstein	California
Small Business and Entrepreneurship	Mary Landrieu	Louisiana
Veterans' Affairs	Daniel Akaka	Hawaii

House Standing Committee chairs

Committee	Chair	State
Agriculture	Collin Peterson	Minnesota
Appropriations	David Obey	Wisconsin
Armed Services	Ike Skelton	Missouri
Budget	John Spratt	South Carolina
Education and Labor	George Miller	California
Energy and Commerce	Henry Waxman	California
Financial Services	Barney Frank	Massachusetts
Foreign Affairs	Howard Berman	California
Homeland Security	Bennie Thompson	Mississippi
Judiciary	John Conyers	Michigan
Natural Resources	Nick Rahall	West Virginia
Oversight and Government Reform	Edolphus Towns	New York
Rules	Louise Slaughter	New York
Science and Technology	Bart Gordon	Tennessee
Small Business	Nydia Velázquez	New York
Transportation and Infrastructure	James Oberstar	Minnesota
Veterans' Affairs	Bob Filner	California
Ways and Means	Charles Rangel	New York

Judicial branch

		President who appointed	Year appointed
Chief Justice	John Roberts	George W. Bush	2005
Associate Justices	John Paul Stevens	Ford	1975
	Antonin Scalia	Reagan	1986
	Anthony Kennedy	Reagan	1988
	David Souter	Bush	1990
	Clarence Thomas	Bush	1991
	Ruth Bader Ginsburg	Clinton	1993
	Stephen Breyer	Clinton	1994
	Samuel Alito	George W. Bush	2006